COLOGNE TRAVEL
2025

Discover the Best of Cologne: Top Sights, Hidden Gems, Insider Tips and Many More

Kenneth O. Pritts

No part of this publication may be reproduced, stored or transmitted in any form or by any means, electronic, mechanical, photocopying, recording, scanning, or otherwise without written permission from the publisher.
It is illegal to copy this book, post it to a website, or distribute it by any other means without permission.

Copyright © 2025 Kenneth O. Pritts

All rights reserved.

DISCLAIMER

Please note that the information provided in this travel guide is subject to change and may not always be accurate or up-to-date.

While every effort has been made to ensure the information provided is reliable, we cannot be held responsible for any errors, omissions, or changes that may occur.

It is recommended that you verify any important information, such as entry requirements, travel restrictions, and local customs, with relevant authorities before embarking on your journey. Additionally, please be aware that traveling can be inherently risky, and we cannot be held liable for any accidents, injuries, illnesses, or losses that may occur during your travels.

COLOGNE

TABLE OF CONTENT

INTRODUCTION 10
Why Visit Cologne in 2025? 11
A Brief History of Cologne 13
How to Use This Guide 15

Chapter 1 19
Getting To Cologne 19
Flights and Airports 19
Tips for Flying into Cologne Bonn Airport 24
Trains and Buses 25
Driving and Car Rentals 28

Chapter 2 35
When to Visit 35
Cologne's Seasons and Weather 35

Chapter 3 41
Getting Around Cologne 41
Public Transportation: Trams, Buses, and Trains 41
Biking Around the City 43

Taxis and Ride-Sharing Services 44

Walking Routes and Neighborhoods 45

Chapter 4 49

Top Attractions in Cologne 49

Cologne Cathedral (Kölner Dom) 49

The Rhine River and Cruises 51

Old Town (Altstadt) 53

Hohenzollern Bridge and Love Locks 55

Roman-Germanic Museum (Römisch-Germanisches Museum) 56

Museum Ludwig 58

Cologne Zoo 59

Flora and Botanical Garden (Flora und Botanischer Garten) 60

Schokoladenmuseum (Chocolate Museum) 61

Chapter 5 63

Hidden Gems in Cologne 63

Local Parks and Gardens 64

Unique Museums and Galleries 65

Off-the-Beaten-Path Neighborhoods 66

Lesser-Known Historical Sites 68

Chapter 6 71

Where to Stay in Cologne 71

Top Hotels for Every Budget 72

Boutique Hotels and Unique Stays 75

Hostels and Budget-Friendly Options 80

Family-Friendly Accommodations 84

Chapter 7 89

Cultural Experiences in Cologne 89

Cologne's Art Scene 89

Cologne Carnival (Karneval) 91

Traditional Music and Performances 92

Local Festivals and Events in 2025 94

Chapter 8 97

Where to Eat and Drink in Cologne 97

Traditional German Cuisine 97

Best Restaurants for Local Food 99

Craft Beer and Breweries 101

Cafés, Bakeries, and Sweets 102

Vegan and Vegetarian Options 104

Chapter 9 107

Day Trips from Cologne 107

Bonn: The Birthplace of Beethoven 107

Düsseldorf: Art, Fashion, and the Rhine 108

Phantasialand: Theme Park Fun 110

Exploring the Moselle Valley and Wine Regions 111

Chapter 10 114

Shopping in Cologne 114

Shopping Streets and Malls 114

Local Markets 116

Luxury Brands and Designer Stores 117

Cologne's Christmas Markets 118

Souvenirs from Cologne 119

Chapter 11 123

Nightlife in Cologne 123

Best Bars and Pubs 123

Live Music Venues and Clubs 124

    Late-Night Dining and Entertainment 126

Chapter 12 129

Cologne for Families 129

    Family-Friendly Attractions 129

    Parks and Playgrounds 131

    Child-Friendly Restaurants and Cafes 133

    Tips for Traveling with Kids 134

Chapter 13 137

Practical Information 137

    Currency and Etiquette in Cologne 137

    Language and Useful Phrases in Cologne 142

    Safety Tips for Travelers in Cologne 148

    Emergency Contacts and Services in Cologne 151

CONCLUSION 155

    Final Thoughts 155

    Recommendations 156

    FAQs 158

INTRODUCTION

Cologne, Germany's fourth-largest city, is a captivating blend of ancient history and modern vibrancy. Nestled along the Rhine River, this metropolis is not just famous for its stunning Gothic architecture but also for its thriving cultural scene, rich traditions, and welcoming atmosphere. Whether you're a history buff, art lover, or simply in search of authentic German experiences, Cologne has something for every traveler.

In 2025, Cologne offers even more reasons to visit, from exciting events and festivals to ongoing development projects that blend old-world charm with new-world convenience.

Why Visit Cologne in 2025?

Cologne is a city that seamlessly merges historical grandeur with a dynamic modern culture, making it a destination that captivates all types of travelers. In 2025, this vibrant city is particularly enticing due to:

- **Exciting Events and Festivals:**

    Cologne's famous Karneval (Carnival) will once again take over the streets with elaborate costumes, music, and lively parades, making 2025 a year to witness this thrilling tradition. Additionally, Cologne will host several international art, music, and food festivals, ensuring that no matter when you visit, there's something to experience.

- **New Attractions and Upgrades:**

    Several landmarks, including the iconic Cologne Cathedral, have undergone renovations, offering a fresh experience for 2025 visitors. New public spaces, exhibitions, and environmentally friendly urban projects will make the city even more inviting.

- **Sustainability Initiatives:**

    With a focus on green travel, Cologne's sustainability projects are transforming the city into a leading destination for eco-conscious travelers. From expanded bike routes to new green spaces, visitors can experience Cologne in a responsible and mindful way.

- **Central Location**:

    Cologne's strategic position in the heart of Europe makes it easily accessible via major airports, train stations, and highways. Whether you're arriving from neighboring countries or beyond, Cologne is perfectly connected for a hassle-free trip.

A Brief History of Cologne

Cologne's history stretches back more than 2,000 years, making it one of Germany's oldest cities. Its story begins in the Roman era when it was founded as Colonia Claudia Ara Agrippinensium in 50 AD, giving it the status of a Roman colony and a significant trade hub. The city's strategic location on the Rhine River played a pivotal role in its growth, helping it become one of the major urban centers of the Holy Roman Empire.

Medieval Cologne

During the Middle Ages, Cologne flourished as a commercial and religious center. The construction of the Cologne Cathedral, one of the most significant Gothic structures in Europe, began in 1248, although it would take over 600 years to complete. By the 14th century, Cologne had established itself as an independent city-state and became a member of the Hanseatic League, further strengthening its economic and political influence.

Cologne in Modern Times

World War II dramatically impacted Cologne, with much of the city being destroyed during Allied bombings. However, its spirit endured, and in the post-war era, Cologne embarked on an ambitious rebuilding effort. The city's historical core was restored, and new modern structures were introduced, creating a unique blend of old and new. Today, Cologne is known for its dynamic economy, robust arts scene, and strong cultural identity.

How to Use This Guide

This travel guide is designed to be a comprehensive resource for exploring Cologne in 2025. Here's how to make the most of it:

1. **Plan Your Trip**

   Whether you're visiting for a few days or an extended stay, this guide provides essential information on when to visit, how to get to Cologne, and the best ways to navigate the city. In the early chapters, you'll find tips on transportation, seasonal highlights, and insider knowledge to ensure you have a smooth journey.

2. **Explore Key Attractions**

   Cologne is brimming with incredible sights, and this guide highlights the top attractions, from the majestic Cologne Cathedral to the lively Old Town. You'll also find hidden gems and lesser-known spots to explore, ensuring that you experience both the popular landmarks and the off-the-beaten-path treasures.

3. Cultural and Culinary Experiences

One of the best ways to connect with Cologne's soul is through its culture and food. Use this guide to discover where to eat and drink, which local dishes to try, and what festivals or events are happening during your visit. You'll also find recommendations for Cologne's art scene, music venues, and local traditions.

4. Tailored Recommendations

Whether you're a solo traveler, visiting with family, or looking for romantic spots, this guide offers tailored suggestions for your trip. Each section includes options for different travel styles and budgets, making it easy to find the experiences that suit your preferences.

5. Practical Information

The guide concludes with essential practical advice, including information about local customs, currency, safety tips, and useful contact numbers. An appendix section provides maps, apps, and further resources to help you navigate and plan your trip efficiently.

Chapter 1
Getting To Cologne

Flights and Airports

Cologne is one of Germany's most accessible cities, thanks to its well-connected international airport and proximity to major European hubs. Whether you're flying from a nearby country or a distant continent, getting to Cologne by air is straightforward and efficient.

Cologne Bonn Airport (CGN)

Cologne Bonn Airport is the city's primary airport and is located just 15 kilometers southeast of the city center. As one of Germany's busiest airports, CGN handles millions of passengers each year and offers a wide range of domestic and international flights. Here's what to know about traveling through Cologne Bonn Airport in 2025:

1. **Terminals**: Cologne Bonn Airport operates two main terminals:

   - **Terminal 1**: Primarily serves full-service airlines such as Lufthansa, Eurowings, and Turkish Airlines.

   - **Terminal 2**: Mostly used by low-cost carriers like Ryanair and Wizz Air, making it a popular choice for budget travelers.

   Both terminals are modern and equipped with all the necessary amenities, including duty-free shopping, restaurants, lounges, and car rental services.

2. **Airlines Serving Cologne Bonn Airport**: CGN is a hub for Eurowings, a popular low-cost airline that offers flights to numerous destinations across Europe, including major cities like Paris, Rome, and London. Other airlines, such as Lufthansa, Ryanair, and Turkish Airlines, also provide extensive flight options to international and domestic locations.

Intercontinental Flights: While Cologne Bonn is not as large as airports in Frankfurt or Munich, it still offers a selection of long-haul flights. Airlines like Turkish Airlines and Qatar Airways operate flights to Asia and the Middle East, while seasonal charter flights may be available to popular vacation destinations in North America and Africa.

3. **Getting to the City from the Airport**: Upon arriving at Cologne Bonn Airport, travelers have several convenient options for getting to the city center:

    - **Train**: The S-Bahn (S13 and S19 lines) runs from the airport's train station directly to Cologne's central station (Köln Hauptbahnhof) in about 15 minutes. Trains are frequent, affordable, and one of the most efficient ways to travel between the airport and downtown.

    - **Bus**: A variety of buses connect the airport to different parts of Cologne and neighboring cities. The SB60 bus is a direct service to Bonn, which is about 30 minutes away.

- **Taxis and Ride-Sharing**: Taxis are available just outside the terminals, and a ride to the city center typically takes 20-25 minutes, depending on traffic. Ride-sharing services like Uber and Bolt also operate in the area, offering an alternative for those looking for more flexibility.

4. **Car Rentals**: For travelers planning to explore Cologne and its surroundings, renting a car is a convenient option. Major car rental companies, such as Hertz, Sixt, Avis, and Europcar, have counters in both terminals. It's recommended to book in advance, especially during busy travel periods like the summer or Christmas season. The airport is connected to major highways, making it easy to embark on road trips to other German cities or nearby countries.

5. **Airport Amenities and Services**: Cologne Bonn Airport offers a range of amenities to ensure a comfortable experience for travelers:

- **Lounges**: For those looking for a quieter space to relax before their flight, the Eurowings Lounge and Airport Business Lounge are available, offering free Wi-Fi, snacks, and comfortable seating.

- **Duty-Free Shopping**: Both terminals feature a variety of duty-free shops, where you can purchase everything from luxury goods and cosmetics to local Cologne specialties like Eau de Cologne.

- **Restaurants and Cafés**: Whether you're in need of a quick snack or a full meal, the airport has plenty of dining options. Popular choices include Kamps (a bakery known for German pastries), Burger King, and Hausmann's (serving traditional German dishes).

Tips for Flying into Cologne Bonn Airport

1. **Book Early for Popular Routes**: As Cologne continues to attract more visitors, flights to and from CGN can become crowded during peak seasons, such as summer and Christmas. If you're planning to visit during these times, it's a good idea to book flights early to secure the best deals and availability.

2. **Check for Budget-Friendly Options**: With Ryanair, Wizz Air, and other low-cost carriers operating out of Terminal 2, Cologne Bonn Airport is a great option for budget travelers. Keep an eye out for special promotions and deals, particularly for short-haul flights across Europe.

3. **Prepare for Security and Customs**: Cologne Bonn Airport has streamlined security and customs processes, but it's always wise to allow yourself enough time, especially if you're flying internationally. Arriving at the airport at least 2-3 hours before departure is recommended for international flights, while domestic travelers can often arrive 1.5-2 hours before.

4. **Connecting Flights**: For those with connecting flights, the layout of Cologne Bonn Airport is compact and easy to navigate. However, it's important to leave enough time between flights, particularly if you need to pass through customs or transfer between Terminals 1 and 2.

5. **Sustainable Travel**: If you're conscious of your carbon footprint, consider offsetting your flight emissions. Cologne Bonn Airport has partnered with several organizations that offer carbon offset programs, allowing travelers to contribute to environmental projects in exchange for offsetting the emissions from their flights.

Trains and Buses

Cologne is one of the best-connected cities in Germany when it comes to public transportation. Whether you're moving around the city or traveling to neighboring regions, the train and bus systems are efficient, affordable, and convenient.

Train Travel in Cologne
Cologne Hauptbahnhof (Central Station):

Cologne's Hauptbahnhof (Central Station) is the primary rail hub in the city and one of the busiest in Germany. It's located near the Cologne Cathedral, making it easily accessible to visitors. From here, you can travel across Germany and Europe.

1. **Long-Distance Trains (ICE, IC, and EC)**: Cologne is served by high-speed trains like the InterCity Express (ICE), which connects to major German cities such as Berlin, Frankfurt, Hamburg, and Munich in just a few hours. The InterCity (IC) and EuroCity (EC) trains offer slower but equally convenient connections to cities throughout Germany and Europe, including Paris, Brussels, Amsterdam, and Zurich. For travelers planning multi-city trips, the extensive long-distance network offers a fast, comfortable option.

2. **Regional Trains (RE and RB)**: Regional Express (RE) and Regional Bahn (RB) trains are perfect for shorter journeys within North Rhine-Westphalia

(NRW) and neighboring regions. These trains connect Cologne with nearby cities like Bonn, Düsseldorf, and Aachen. They also stop at smaller towns, providing access to the scenic Rhineland area.

3. **S-Bahn (Commuter Trains)**: The S-Bahn network serves Cologne and its suburbs. Lines like S6, S11, S12, S13, and S19 link key districts in Cologne with nearby areas such as the airport, neighboring towns, and regions. The S-Bahn is ideal for daily commuting and short journeys, offering a fast and affordable way to move around the city.

Bus Travel in Cologne

Cologne's bus network complements its train system, providing extensive coverage throughout the city and neighboring areas.

1. **City Buses**: City buses run frequently and connect areas that are not directly served by the S-Bahn or U-Bahn networks. These buses are reliable, running on a regular schedule, and stop at key landmarks, residential areas, and shopping centers. Some buses

also operate late into the night, making them a practical option for getting around after hours.

2. **Long-Distance Buses**: For travelers on a budget, long-distance buses are an affordable alternative to trains for intercity travel. Companies like FlixBus offer routes to major cities across Germany and Europe, including Berlin, Amsterdam, and Brussels. The Cologne Bonn Airport bus terminal is a major hub for these services.

Driving and Car Rentals

While Cologne boasts excellent public transportation, some travelers may prefer the flexibility of renting a car to explore the city and its surrounding regions.

Renting a Car in Cologne

1. **Major Rental Companies**: Cologne has several major car rental companies, including Hertz, Europcar, Sixt, and Avis, which offer a wide range of vehicles. Most of these companies have offices at Cologne Bonn Airport, the central train station, and various locations around the city. Renting a car is a

convenient option for travelers planning day trips or excursions beyond Cologne, especially to rural areas or nearby cities like Bonn or Düsseldorf.

2. **Road Conditions and Driving in Cologne**: Cologne's road network is well-developed, but like many large European cities, it can experience heavy traffic, especially during rush hours. The city has several one-way streets and restricted areas, so it's important to use a GPS or map service to navigate efficiently. Parking is available throughout the city, with several public garages and parking lots near major attractions. However, be aware that street parking can be limited in busy areas, and fees often apply.

3. **Day Trips by Car**: Renting a car allows travelers to visit nearby destinations at their own pace. Popular day trips from Cologne include exploring the wine regions along the Rhine River, visiting the medieval castles of Burg Eltz and Marksburg, or taking a scenic drive to the nearby Eifel Mountains.

Driving Tips for Visitors

- **Low Emission Zones (Umweltzone)**: Like many German cities, Cologne has a low-emission zone in its city center. Cars must display a green emissions sticker to enter these areas. Most rental cars will already have this sticker, but it's always worth checking when picking up your vehicle.

- **Autobahn Etiquette**: If you plan to drive on the German Autobahn, remember that while some sections have no speed limit, many do. Pay close attention to posted limits, especially near construction zones and urban areas.

- **Fuel**: Gas stations are plentiful, but prices can vary. It's advisable to refuel at stations outside city centers or along major highways for better rates.

Sustainable Travel Options

Cologne is increasingly focused on sustainable travel, with several green initiatives in place to promote eco-friendly options for both locals and visitors.

Biking in Cologne

1. **Bike-Friendly Infrastructure**: Cologne is a bike-friendly city with dedicated cycling lanes and bike paths running through many of its neighborhoods. The flat landscape makes it easy for cyclists to navigate the city, whether you're commuting, sightseeing, or exploring nearby parks.

2. **Bike Rentals and Sharing Services**: Visitors can rent bikes from a number of providers, including Nextbike, a popular bike-sharing service available across Cologne. There are numerous docking stations throughout the city, especially near tourist attractions, parks, and public transport hubs. Rentals are affordable, and bikes can be picked up and dropped off at different locations, offering great flexibility.

3. **Bike Tours**: For those who prefer a guided experience, Cologne offers several bike tour operators that lead excursions around the city. These tours often cover major landmarks like the Cologne Cathedral, Hohenzollern Bridge, and scenic routes along the Rhine River.

Public Transportation's Green Initiatives

Cologne's public transport network is working to reduce its environmental impact by introducing more eco-friendly vehicles and systems.

1. **Electric and Hybrid Buses**: The city has begun transitioning its bus fleet to include electric and hybrid buses, which help reduce emissions and noise pollution. This shift is part of Cologne's broader goal to become a more sustainable city.

2. **Renewable Energy in Rail Systems**: Cologne's S-Bahn and U-Bahn networks increasingly rely on renewable energy sources, contributing to a greener transportation system. The city is investing in

energy-efficient infrastructure to reduce the carbon footprint of public transport.

Walking in Cologne

Cologne is also a walkable city, with many of its major attractions located within a compact area. Walking is an enjoyable and sustainable way to explore the Old Town, Rhine promenade, and surrounding neighborhoods. Pedestrian zones and parks make it easy to navigate the city on foot, with plenty of sights and cafes along the way.

Eco-Friendly Accommodations

Cologne has several hotels and guesthouses that prioritize sustainability. Many accommodations are committed to energy efficiency, recycling programs, and using locally sourced products. For eco-conscious travelers, staying in these establishments helps reduce the environmental impact of your trip.

Chapter 2
When to Visit

Cologne's Seasons and Weather

Cologne experiences a temperate oceanic climate, characterized by mild winters, warm summers, and a fair amount of rainfall throughout the year. Understanding the city's seasons and weather patterns can help travelers plan their visit effectively and make the most of their time in this vibrant German city.

1. Spring (March to May)

- **Weather Overview**: Spring in Cologne is a delightful time as the city shakes off the chill of winter. Temperatures gradually rise, with average daytime highs ranging from 10°C (50°F) in March to around 20°C (68°F) by May. Nights can still be chilly, especially in March, when temperatures can drop to around 1°C (34°F).

- **Rainfall**: Spring can be quite rainy, with March and April experiencing more precipitation than

May. Travelers should be prepared for occasional showers and pack an umbrella or light rain jacket.

- **What to Expect**: As the days lengthen and flowers bloom, spring is a lovely season to explore Cologne. Many outdoor events and festivals begin during this time, including the famous Cologne Carnival (though it typically peaks in February or early March), and the city's parks, such as Rheinpark and Stadtgarten, come alive with picnics and outdoor activities.

2. **Summer (June to August)**
- **Weather Overview**: Summer is warm and often pleasant, making it a popular time for tourists. Average high temperatures range from 22°C (72°F) in June to around 26°C (79°F) in July and August. However, heatwaves can occasionally push temperatures above 30°C (86°F).

- **Rainfall**: Summer in Cologne tends to be wetter than spring, with June being one of the rainiest months. Thunderstorms are not uncommon but usually pass quickly.

- **What to Expect**: Summer is vibrant in Cologne, with numerous outdoor festivals, concerts, and events. The Cologne Pride Parade (Christopher Street Day) takes place in July, drawing thousands of visitors. It's an excellent time for outdoor dining along the Rhine River, exploring open-air markets, or taking part in summer fairs.

3. Autumn (September to November)

- **Weather Overview**: Autumn brings a gradual drop in temperatures, with September still enjoying mild weather (averaging around 20°C or 68°F), while November can be quite chilly, with average highs of about 8°C (46°F). Nights can become quite cold, so layering is advisable.

- **Rainfall**: Rainfall increases in autumn, particularly in October and November. Travelers should be prepared for wet and cool conditions, especially later in the season.

- **What to Expect**: Autumn is a beautiful time to visit Cologne, as the changing leaves create stunning scenery in the city's parks and along the Rhine. The Cologne Wine Festival in September celebrates the region's rich wine culture, while the start of the Christmas market season in late November offers enchanting holiday experiences.

4. Winter (December to February)

- **Weather Overview**: Winters in Cologne can be cold, with average high temperatures around 5°C (41°F) in December and February. January tends to be the coldest month, with temperatures sometimes dipping below freezing at night.

- **Rainfall and Snow**: Rainfall is relatively low in winter, but snow is possible, especially in January and February, although significant accumulation is rare. Overcast skies and short daylight hours are typical during this season.

- **What to Expect**: Winter transforms Cologne into a festive wonderland, particularly during the

Christmas season. The city is famous for its Christmas markets, with the largest one held at Cologne Cathedral. Visitors can enjoy traditional foods, crafts, and holiday cheer. The festive lights and decorations throughout the city add to the magical atmosphere.

Travel Tips for Cologne's Weather

1. **Layering is Key**: Given the variability of Cologne's weather, particularly in spring and autumn, layering is essential. Lightweight, breathable fabrics are ideal for summer, while warmer layers are recommended for cooler months.

2. **Pack for Rain**: Regardless of the season, a compact umbrella or waterproof jacket is advisable, as rain can occur unexpectedly.

3. **Seasonal Events**: Plan your visit around seasonal events that match your interests. From the vibrant summer festivals to the enchanting Christmas markets, each season offers unique experiences.

4. **Climate Considerations**: Check the weather forecast before your trip to ensure you're prepared for any unexpected weather conditions, particularly if you plan outdoor activities.

5. **Public Transport**: Cologne's public transport system is excellent, making it easy to navigate the city regardless of the weather. During rainy days or cold winters, utilizing trams and buses can keep you comfortable.

Chapter 3
Getting Around Cologne

Cologne is a vibrant city with a well-developed transportation network, making it easy for visitors to explore its many attractions. Whether you prefer public transport, biking, taxis, or walking, you'll find convenient options for getting around.

Public Transportation: Trams, Buses, and Trains

Cologne boasts an extensive and efficient public transportation system, including trams, buses, and trains. The KVB (Kölner Verkehrs-Betriebe) operates most of the public transport services, ensuring that both locals and tourists can easily access the city's main attractions and neighborhoods.

1. **Trams:** The tram network in Cologne is one of the most effective ways to navigate the city. With numerous lines connecting key areas, trams provide

quick and frequent service. Notable tram lines include:

- **Line 1**: Runs from the northern suburbs to the southern parts of the city, passing major attractions such as the Cologne Cathedral and the Old Town.
- **Line 7 and 9**: Connects the city center to the vibrant neighborhoods of Ehrenfeld and Deutz.

Trams generally run every 5-10 minutes, making them a reliable option for getting around.

2. **Buses**: The bus network complements the tram system, reaching areas that are not directly served by tram lines. Buses operate frequently and connect residential neighborhoods, shopping areas, and attractions. Many buses also run late into the night, providing service for evening events and nightlife.

3. **S-Bahn and Regional Trains**: The S-Bahn (commuter train) network connects Cologne to the surrounding regions and nearby cities. Lines S6, S11,

and S12 provide direct access to neighboring towns and are an excellent option for day trips. Regional trains also connect to cities like Bonn, Düsseldorf, and Aachen.

4. **Tickets and Fares**: Tickets for public transport can be purchased at ticket machines located in tram stops and train stations. Various ticket options are available, including single-journey tickets, day passes, and multi-ride tickets. It's essential to validate your ticket before boarding, as inspections are common.

Biking Around the City

Biking is a popular and eco-friendly way to explore Cologne. The city has made significant strides in becoming more bike-friendly, with dedicated bike lanes and paths throughout many neighborhoods.

1. **Bike Rentals**: Visitors can rent bikes from several providers, including Nextbike, which operates a bike-sharing system. Bikes can be rented from various docking stations across the city and returned at

different locations, making it convenient to explore Cologne on two wheels.

2. **Cycling Infrastructure**: Cologne has invested in cycling infrastructure, including well-marked bike lanes and parking facilities. Biking along the Rhine River promenade is particularly enjoyable, offering beautiful views of the river and the Cologne skyline.

3. **Bike Tours**: For those who prefer a guided experience, several companies offer bike tours of the city. These tours often cover key landmarks, hidden gems, and scenic routes, providing a unique perspective on Cologne.

Taxis and Ride-Sharing Services

While public transport is widely used, taxis and ride-sharing services are also available for those who prefer a more direct mode of transport.

1. **Taxis**: Taxis are readily available throughout the city, and taxi ranks can be found near major train stations, hotels, and popular attractions. Fares are

metered, and rides can be booked via phone or hailed on the street.

2. **Ride-Sharing Services**: Services like Uber and Free Now operate in Cologne, offering an alternative to traditional taxis. These platforms allow users to book rides conveniently through their mobile apps, providing price estimates and tracking options.

3. **Airport Transfers**: For travelers arriving at Cologne Bonn Airport, taxis and ride-sharing services are available for direct transfers to the city center or other destinations.

Walking Routes and Neighborhoods

Walking is a delightful way to experience Cologne's charm and character. The city's compact size makes it easy to explore on foot, with many attractions located within walking distance of each other.

1. **Scenic Walking Routes**: Visitors can enjoy scenic walks along the Rhine River, where they can take in views of the Cologne Cathedral, Hohenzollern

Bridge, and the vibrant riverside promenade. The Old Town (Altstadt) is another pedestrian-friendly area with narrow streets, historic buildings, and plenty of cafes and shops.

2. **Neighborhood Exploration**: Cologne has a variety of neighborhoods, each with its unique vibe. Here are a few notable areas to explore on foot:

    - **Old Town (Altstadt)**: Home to iconic landmarks, cobblestone streets, and lively beer gardens. Don't miss the historic Alter Markt and Heumarkt squares.

    - **Belgian Quarter (Belgisches Viertel)**: Known for its trendy boutiques, cafes, and vibrant nightlife, this area is perfect for strolling and people-watching.

    - **Ehrenfeld**: A multicultural neighborhood filled with street art, independent shops, and a diverse food scene. It's a great place to explore for a taste of local life.

3. **Walking Tours**: Guided walking tours are available for those who want to delve deeper into Cologne's history, culture, and hidden gems. These tours often include stops at significant landmarks, local eateries, and historical sites, providing insight into the city's rich heritage.

Chapter 4
Top Attractions in Cologne

Cologne offers a wealth of attractions that combine its rich history, vibrant culture, and stunning architecture. Whether you're drawn to Gothic cathedrals, scenic rivers, or world-class museums, here are the top attractions you should not miss when visiting this dynamic city.

Cologne Cathedral (Kölner Dom)

Cologne Cathedral is the city's most famous and iconic landmark, recognized for its stunning Gothic architecture and twin spires that dominate the skyline. This UNESCO World Heritage Site is not only a symbol of Cologne but also one of the largest cathedrals in Europe.

- **What to See**: Inside the cathedral, visitors can marvel at the magnificent stained-glass windows and the Shrine of the Three Kings, a golden reliquary believed to hold the remains of the Biblical Magi. For a more adventurous experience, climb the 533 steps to the top of the south tower for panoramic views of the city.

- **Location**: The Cologne Cathedral is located at Domkloster 4, right next to the Köln Hauptbahnhof (Cologne Central Station), making it easily accessible from any part of the city. It is the heart of Cologne's historic center.

The Rhine River and Cruises

The Rhine River is the lifeblood of Cologne, and its banks are filled with life and activity. The riverside promenades provide an ideal setting for leisurely strolls, offering great views of both the modern and historic parts of the city. The Rhine itself is best explored through a river cruise, a popular way to enjoy Cologne from a different perspective.

- **What to Do**: Cruises along the Rhine range from short sightseeing trips that showcase Cologne's most famous landmarks to longer excursions that explore the surrounding Rhineland. These cruises offer views of the Cologne Cathedral, the Hohenzollern Bridge, and Cologne's historic Old Town.

- **Location**: Cruises typically depart from piers near the Old Town, along the Rheinuferpromenade (Rhine promenade), which is accessible from several points, including Frankenwerft and Kennedy-Ufer.

Old Town (Altstadt)

Cologne's Old Town (Altstadt) is the heart of the city's historical and cultural heritage. It is characterized by cobblestone streets, medieval houses, and picturesque squares, making it a favorite area for tourists. The Old Town's lively atmosphere, along with its traditional breweries, beer gardens, and restaurants, gives visitors a taste of the authentic Cologne experience.

- **What to Explore**: Wander through the narrow alleys and colorful houses that line the Rhine River. The Alter Markt and Heumarkt squares are central gathering spots filled with cafes and bars, particularly popular for enjoying Cologne's signature Kölsch beer. Be sure to visit St. Martin's Church, a Romanesque church that dominates the skyline with its imposing presence.

- **Location**: The Old Town is located along the Rhine River, just south of the Cologne Cathedral. Key streets include Am Hof and Salzgasse, which lead to the main squares.

Hohenzollern Bridge and Love Locks

The Hohenzollern Bridge is both a functional and symbolic landmark in Cologne. While it serves as one of the busiest railway bridges in Germany, it's equally known for the thousands of "love locks" that couples from all over the world attach to the bridge as a symbol of eternal love.

- **What to See**: A walk across the Hohenzollern Bridge provides one of the best views of the Cologne Cathedral and the Rhine River. Many visitors take the opportunity to leave their own lock on the bridge, contributing to a romantic tradition. At night, the bridge and the Cathedral create a breathtaking illuminated backdrop.

- **Location**: The bridge spans the Rhine, connecting Cologne's Old Town to the Deutz district. It begins just behind the Cologne Cathedral, making it easy to visit after exploring the area.

Roman-Germanic Museum (Römisch-Germanisches Museum)

Cologne has a deep-rooted Roman history, and the Roman-Germanic Museum offers a fascinating glimpse into this ancient past. The museum houses an impressive collection of Roman artifacts that have been discovered in and around Cologne, which was once the Roman city of Colonia Claudia Ara Agrippinensium.

- **What to See**: The museum's most famous piece is the Mosaic of Dionysus, an intricately detailed floor mosaic from a Roman villa, which is displayed in its original location. The museum also features ancient Roman glassware, pottery, jewelry, and statues, providing insight into daily life during Roman times. Don't miss the well-preserved Roman Burial Chamber, another highlight of the museum.

- **Location**: The Roman-Germanic Museum is located at Roncalliplatz 4, right next to the Cologne Cathedral. This makes it a convenient stop for those visiting the city's central attractions.

Museum Ludwig

For modern art enthusiasts, Museum Ludwig is a must-visit destination in Cologne. The museum is known for its outstanding collection of contemporary art, with a special focus on Pop Art and 20th-century movements. It also houses one of the largest collections of works by Pablo Picasso in Europe.

- **What to Explore**: The museum boasts an impressive array of Pop Art pieces by artists like Andy Warhol, Roy Lichtenstein, and Jasper Johns. Its permanent collection also includes works from German Expressionism, Surrealism, and Abstract Expressionism, offering a comprehensive look at some of the most influential art movements of the 20th century.

- **Location**: Museum Ludwig is located at Heinrich-Böll-Platz, just a short walk from the Cologne Cathedral and the Rhine River. Its central location makes it easy to combine a visit to the museum with other nearby attractions.

Cologne Zoo

Founded in 1860, Cologne Zoo is one of the oldest and most respected zoos in Germany. It's home to over 10,000 animals from across the globe, making it a fun and educational destination for families and animal lovers alike.

- **What to See**: Don't miss the Elephant Park, one of the largest in Europe, and the Aquarium, which features marine life from around the world. The zoo also has an impressive collection of primates, reptiles, and exotic birds.

- **Location**: Riehler Str. 173, near the Flora Botanical Garden.

Flora and Botanical Garden (Flora und Botanischer Garten)

Adjacent to the Cologne Zoo, the Flora and Botanical Garden is a peaceful retreat from the bustling city. Spread over 11.5 hectares, it's the largest and oldest park in Cologne, featuring thousands of plant species from around the world.

- **What to Explore**: Visitors can stroll through beautiful landscapes, including a rose garden, tropical greenhouses, and rare plant collections. The Flora Pavilion, a stunning 19th-century glasshouse, is a popular venue for events and exhibitions.

- **Location**: Amsterdamer Str. 34, next to the Cologne Zoo.

Schokoladenmuseum (Chocolate Museum)

The Chocolate Museum is a treat for chocolate lovers of all ages. It traces the history of chocolate, from its origins with the ancient Mayans and Aztecs to its role in European history and culture.

- **What to See**: The museum features live demonstrations of chocolate production, interactive exhibits, and a large chocolate fountain that visitors can sample. There's also a shop where you can buy freshly made chocolates.

- **Location**: Am Schokoladenmuseum 1A, on the Rheinauhafen peninsula, just south of the Old Town.

Chapter 5
Hidden Gems in Cologne

Cologne is a city with world-famous landmarks, but beyond the well-trodden paths of the Cathedral and the Old Town, there are many hidden gems waiting to be discovered. From tranquil parks to quirky museums, exploring Cologne's lesser-known spots will give you a deeper appreciation of the city's character and charm.

Local Parks and Gardens

Cologne is home to numerous parks and green spaces that offer peaceful retreats away from the bustling city center. These local parks are perfect for relaxing, picnicking, or simply enjoying nature.

- **Stadtwald (City Forest)**: Located in the western part of Cologne, the Stadtwald is a vast urban forest with scenic lakes, walking paths, and plenty of wildlife. It's a popular spot for jogging, cycling, and outdoor sports. The forest's serene atmosphere makes it ideal for escaping the city's hustle and bustle.

- **Volksgarten**: Situated south of the city center, the Volksgarten is a beautiful park with a large pond where you can rent paddleboats. It's also a popular spot for locals to relax, have barbecues, and enjoy outdoor concerts in the summer.

- **Flora and Botanical Garden**: While the Botanical Garden is well-known, the adjacent Flora park often flies under the radar. It's a lovely, manicured garden with elegant pathways, fountains, and a historic greenhouse. This park offers a peaceful setting for a quiet stroll and is a must for plant lovers.

Unique Museums and Galleries

Cologne boasts a wide range of museums and galleries, but some of the more unusual options often get overlooked by visitors. These hidden cultural gems offer a different perspective on art, history, and design.

- **Kolumba Museum**: This museum, run by the Archdiocese of Cologne, is a true hidden gem. It blends contemporary art with ancient artifacts in a stunning modern building that incorporates the ruins of a former Gothic church. The minimalist design of the museum complements its collection, which spans various art forms and periods.

- **Odysseum Adventure Museum**: A museum that's often overlooked by tourists, the Odysseum is an interactive science museum designed for families and children. It combines fun exhibits with educational activities in the fields of science, technology, and history. It's a great off-the-beaten-path destination for families traveling with kids.

- **German Sport and Olympic Museum**: Tucked away in the Rheinauhafen area, this museum chronicles the history of sport in Germany and beyond. It's an interactive and engaging museum, where you can try your hand at various sports and explore exhibits on Olympic history, soccer, and other athletic events.

Off-the-Beaten-Path Neighborhoods

While the Old Town and city center are the most popular areas for visitors, Cologne has several off-the-beaten-path neighborhoods that are worth exploring. These districts are full of local charm, unique shops, and vibrant street life.

- **Ehrenfeld**: Located west of the city center, Ehrenfeld is a trendy, multicultural neighborhood known for its street art, hip cafes, and alternative culture. This area is perfect for those who want to experience the edgier, more creative side of Cologne. Don't miss the colorful murals and graffiti that adorn the walls of Ehrenfeld's buildings.

- **Belgisches Viertel (Belgian Quarter)**: This stylish district is famous for its independent boutiques, galleries, and cool bars. It's a hub of creativity and a hotspot for Cologne's young, trendy crowd. In the evening, the Belgian Quarter comes alive with locals enjoying the many chic cafes and restaurants that line the streets.

- **Südstadt**: Cologne's Südstadt neighborhood, located south of the Old Town, has a laid-back, bohemian vibe. The area is known for its historic buildings, relaxed atmosphere, and an array of quirky shops and local eateries. **Chlodwigplatz**, the central square in Südstadt, is a great place to people-watch while sipping a coffee or a Kölsch.

Lesser-Known Historical Sites

Cologne's rich history goes far beyond its famous Cathedral and Roman roots. Several lesser-known historical sites offer a deeper understanding of the city's past and are often overlooked by visitors.

- **St. Maria im Kapitol**: One of the oldest and most historically significant churches in Cologne, St. Maria im Kapitol is a Romanesque church built on the site of an ancient Roman temple. It's less crowded than the Cathedral but equally fascinating, with beautiful medieval architecture and ancient relics inside.

- **Eigelstein Torburg**: This ancient city gate dates back to the Middle Ages and is one of the last remaining structures from Cologne's medieval fortifications. Located in the Eigelstein district, the gate stands as a reminder of the city's fortified past and is a great spot to explore for history enthusiasts.

- **Melaten Cemetery**: Located in the Lindenthal district, Melaten Cemetery is more than just a burial ground – it's a historical landmark filled with stunning sculptures and tombs. Many of Cologne's famous citizens are buried here, and walking through the cemetery feels like wandering through an open-air museum. It's a peaceful yet fascinating place to visit.

Chapter 6
Where to Stay in Cologne

Cologne offers a wide range of accommodations to suit every traveler's needs, whether you're seeking luxury, boutique experiences, budget-friendly options, or family-oriented stays. This vibrant city has everything from five-star hotels with breathtaking views to quirky hostels and unique accommodations.

Top Hotels for Every Budget

Cologne's diverse range of hotels ensures that there's something for every type of traveler, whether you're seeking high-end luxury or mid-range comfort.

1. Excelsior Hotel Ernst (Luxury)

Situated right next to the iconic Cologne Cathedral, Excelsior Hotel Ernst is one of the city's most prestigious five-star hotels. Known for its timeless elegance, impeccable service, and luxurious ambiance, the hotel has been welcoming guests for over 150 years. The hotel's Michelin-starred restaurant, Taku, offers gourmet Asian cuisine, making it an excellent dining option for food lovers.

- **Location**: Trankgasse 1-5, next to Cologne Central Station (Köln Hauptbahnhof) and the Cathedral.
- **Why Stay Here**: Perfect for travelers who desire luxury and historical significance, with easy access to the city's top attractions.

2. Hyatt Regency Cologne (Luxury)

Overlooking the Rhine River, this five-star hotel offers a blend of modern luxury and stunning panoramic views of the Cologne Cathedral. The hotel's contemporary design is complemented by its excellent amenities, including a state-of-the-art spa and riverside terrace. The Glashaus Restaurant inside the hotel serves international cuisine while offering spectacular views of the river and Cathedral.

- **Location**: Kennedy-Ufer 2A, across the river from Cologne's Old Town, in the Deutz district.
- **Why Stay Here**: Ideal for travelers seeking luxury accommodations with breathtaking views and convenient access to both sides of the river.

3. Hotel Mondial am Dom Cologne (Mid-Range)

This four-star hotel offers a great balance of comfort, convenience, and affordability. Located steps from the Cologne Cathedral and the Old Town, it's perfect for those wanting to stay in the heart of the city. The hotel's modern rooms and amenities ensure a comfortable stay, while its proximity to the city's top attractions makes it ideal for sightseeing.

- **Location**: Kurt-Hackenberg-Platz 1, near the Cologne Cathedral and Museum Ludwig.
- **Why Stay Here**: Great for mid-range travelers who want modern comfort and a central location near major attractions.

4. Hotel Lyskirchen (Mid-Range)

This boutique hotel, located near the Chocolate Museum in the Rheinauhafen district, offers a chic and modern atmosphere with reasonable pricing. The hotel's stylish décor and welcoming service make it a favorite among business and leisure travelers. The indoor pool and fitness center add to its appeal.

- **Location**: Filzengraben 26-32, close to the Rheinauhafen and Chocolate Museum.
- **Why Stay Here**: A perfect blend of style and comfort, close to Cologne's scenic riverside and cultural attractions.

5. Motel One Köln-Neumarkt (Budget-Friendly)

For those seeking budget-friendly yet stylish accommodations, Motel One offers a trendy design at an affordable price. Located near Neumarkt, a popular shopping and transport hub, the hotel provides easy access to Cologne's shopping districts and the Old Town. Its modern rooms are compact but functional, making it a great choice for budget-conscious travelers.

- **Location**: Cäcilienstraße 32, near **Neumarkt**.
- **Why Stay Here**: Budget-conscious travelers looking for style, convenience, and proximity to public transportation and shopping.

Boutique Hotels and Unique Stays

Cologne's boutique hotels offer a more intimate, stylish experience, providing a personalized touch for travelers who appreciate unique accommodations. These hotels stand out for their character, creativity, and exceptional service.

1. 25hours Hotel The Circle

One of the trendiest boutique hotels in Cologne, 25hours Hotel The Circle is located in a former bank building with retro-futuristic design elements. The circular shape of the building adds to its distinctiveness, and the rooms are creatively designed with mid-century modern décor. The hotel's rooftop bar offers stunning views of the Cologne skyline, making it a popular spot for evening drinks.

- **Location**: Im Klapperhof 22-24, near the Belgian Quarter.
- **Why Stay Here**: Perfect for travelers seeking a quirky, modern stay with Instagram-worthy interiors and panoramic city views.

2. Qvest Hideaway

Housed in a neo-Gothic building, Qvest Hideaway blends contemporary design with historical architecture. The hotel's interior is a mix of mid-century modern furniture, contemporary art, and antiques, creating a museum-like atmosphere. Each room is unique, and the hotel also serves as a cultural hotspot for art and design lovers.

- **Location**: Gereonskloster 12, close to St. Gereon Basilica.
- **Why Stay Here**: Ideal for art and design enthusiasts who appreciate historical buildings with a modern twist.

3. Humboldt1 Palais-Hotel & Bar

This small, chic boutique hotel offers a truly intimate experience. Located near the Cologne Cathedral, Humboldt1 is a hidden gem in the city center, providing luxury on a smaller scale. The hotel's interiors are designed with plush furnishings, and its on-site bar is perfect for a relaxed evening.

- **Location**: Kupfergasse 10, in the Altstadt-Nord district.
- **Why Stay Here**: Great for travelers seeking an intimate, luxury boutique experience close to Cologne's main attractions.

4. Hotel Marsil

A hip, independently-run boutique hotel, Hotel Marsil combines artistic charm with a laid-back atmosphere. Each room is uniquely designed with eclectic furniture and décor, giving it a distinctly creative vibe. The hotel also doubles as an art gallery, showcasing works from local artists.

- **Location**: Marsilstein 29, near the Südstadt.
- **Why Stay Here**: Perfect for creative travelers who appreciate art, design, and quirky accommodations.

5. Lint Hotel

A small, cozy boutique hotel located in Cologne's Old Town, Lint Hotel is housed in a charming historic building. With only a handful of rooms, it offers an intimate, quiet stay amidst the lively streets of the Old Town. The hotel's blend of traditional charm and modern comforts makes it a hidden gem.

- **Location**: Lintgasse 7, in the Altstadt, near the Great St. Martin Church.

- **Why Stay Here**: Ideal for travelers looking for a quiet, cozy stay in the heart of Cologne's Old Town.

6. Mauritius Hotel & Therme

A unique option for relaxation-seekers, Mauritius Hotel features an in-house thermal spa with multiple pools, saunas, and wellness treatments. Guests can unwind after a day of sightseeing in the hotel's extensive wellness facilities, making it a great choice for those wanting a mix of city exploration and relaxation.

- **Location**: Mauritiuskirchplatz 3-11, near the Rudolfplatz.
- **Why Stay Here**: Perfect for travelers seeking a wellness retreat with the convenience of staying in a central location.

Hostels and Budget-Friendly Options

For backpackers and budget-conscious travelers, Cologne offers a variety of affordable hostels that provide comfort, convenience, and the opportunity to meet fellow travelers.

1. Die Wohngemeinschaft

One of Cologne's most popular hostels, Die Wohngemeinschaft is located in the trendy Belgian Quarter. It offers themed dormitory and private rooms, each with its own unique design. The hostel's cozy bar and lounge area are great for meeting other travelers, while the neighborhood's vibrant cafes and nightlife provide plenty of entertainment.

- **Location**: Richard-Wagner-Straße 39, in the Belgian Quarter.
- **Why Stay Here**: Ideal for social travelers seeking a stylish, lively hostel experience in a hip neighborhood.

2. Pathpoint Cologne Backpacker Hostel

Located in a former church, Pathpoint Cologne is a central and budget-friendly option just a short walk from the **Cologne Cathedral**. It features dormitory rooms, a large common area, and a fully equipped kitchen, making it a practical choice for travelers who want to be close to the city's top sights.

- **Location**: Allie-Prey-Straße 7, near Cologne Central Station.
- **Why Stay Here**: Great for budget travelers who want to stay near the heart of Cologne's main attractions.

3. Black Sheep Hostel

Situated in the lively Südstadt district, Black Sheep Hostel offers a laid-back, creative atmosphere with colorful rooms and friendly staff. The hostel is close to popular nightlife spots, and its central location makes it a great base for exploring the city.

- **Location**: Barbarossaplatz, in the Südstadt.

- **Why Stay Here**: Perfect for budget-conscious travelers who enjoy a fun, bohemian vibe with easy access to nightlife.

4. Station Hostel for Backpackers

Located right next to Cologne Central Station, this hostel is all about convenience. Station Hostel offers a range of dormitory and private rooms at affordable prices, along with a lively bar that hosts regular events. Its proximity to both the station and the Cologne Cathedral makes it a great choice for those wanting to explore the city with ease.

- **Location**: Marzellenstraße 44-56, near Cologne Central Station.
- **Why Stay Here**: Ideal for travelers prioritizing location and budget, especially those using public transport.

5. SMARTY Cologne City Center

A contemporary, budget-friendly hostel located in the heart of Cologne City Center, SMARTY offers modern dormitory and private rooms, free Wi-Fi, and a communal kitchen. Its central location makes it easy to explore the city's sights on foot or via public transport.

- **Location**: Engelbertstraße 33-35, in the Neustadt-Süd district.
- **Why Stay Here**: Great for budget travelers who want modern facilities and easy access to Cologne's main attractions.

6. Hostel Köln

A well-maintained, affordable hostel located near the Rudolfplatz, Hostel Köln offers clean, comfortable accommodations in a friendly environment. The hostel provides both dormitory and private rooms, and its central location makes it a great base for exploring the city.

- **Location**: Marsilstein 29, near the Rudolfplatz.
- **Why Stay Here**: A solid choice for travelers looking for a reliable, budget-friendly stay in a central area.

Family-Friendly Accommodations

Traveling with family? Cologne offers several family-friendly hotels and accommodations that cater to the needs of both parents and children. These hotels provide larger rooms, family amenities, and child-friendly services, ensuring a comfortable stay for everyone:

1. Novotel Köln City

This modern hotel is located along the Rhine River, close to the Chocolate Museum and within walking distance of the city center. Novotel is known for its family-friendly facilities, including spacious rooms, a children's play area, and free breakfast for kids.

- **Location**: Bayenstraße 51, near the Rheinauhafen district.

- **Why Stay Here**: Great for families looking for a central location with easy access to kid-friendly attractions like the Chocolate Museum.

2. Radisson Blu Hotel Cologne

A sleek, modern hotel located near the Koelnmesse exhibition center and the Lanxess Arena, the Radisson Blu offers family rooms, a large breakfast buffet, and close proximity to the Cologne Zoo and Botanical Garden.

- **Location**: Messe Kreisel 3, near the Deutz district.
- **Why Stay Here**: Ideal for families attending events at Koelnmesse or exploring the city's family-friendly attractions.

3. Holiday Inn Express Cologne – Mülheim

Located outside the city center, this hotel offers family rooms and a free breakfast buffet, making it a great option for families on a budget. The Holiday Inn

Express provides easy access to the Odysseum Science Adventure and is just a short drive from the city center.

- **Location**: Tiefentalstraße 72, in the Mülheim district.
- **Why Stay Here**: Budget-friendly option with spacious family rooms and proximity to family attractions like the Odysseum.

4. Jugendherberge Köln-Deutz (Cologne-Deutz Youth Hostel)

This modern youth hostel offers family rooms and is located just across the Rhine from the Old Town. It's a short walk to the Hohenzollern Bridge and Cologne Cathedral, making it a convenient option for families who want affordable accommodation with easy access to the city's attractions.

- **Location**: Siegesstraße 5, near Deutz.
- **Why Stay Here**: Great for families seeking budget accommodations close to central Cologne with plenty of kid-friendly activities nearby.

5. NH Collection Köln Mediapark

Located in the Mediapark district, this upscale hotel offers spacious rooms and suites ideal for families. The hotel has a park-like setting with a lake nearby, making it a peaceful escape from the bustling city center while still being within easy reach of the main attractions.

- **Location**: Im Mediapark 8b, near the Cologne Tower.
- **Why Stay Here**: Ideal for families who want a tranquil setting without sacrificing proximity to the city center.

Chapter 7
Cultural Experiences in Cologne

Cologne is a city where tradition meets modernity, offering a rich cultural scene that spans art, music, festivals, and more. Whether you're interested in visiting world-class galleries, enjoying the lively atmosphere of Cologne Carnival, or experiencing local traditions, the city offers a diverse array of cultural experiences.

Cologne's Art Scene

Cologne's art scene is dynamic and diverse, ranging from contemporary art galleries to historical exhibitions. The city is home to several renowned museums and a thriving gallery culture that draws art enthusiasts from around the world.

- **Museum Ludwig**: Located near the Cologne Cathedral, Museum Ludwig is o`ne of the most important museums of modern art in Europe. It features an extensive collection of 20th- and 21st-century art, including works by Picasso, Andy Warhol, and Roy Lichtenstein. In 2025, the museum is expected to host several temporary exhibitions showcasing both local and international artists.

- **Wallraf-Richartz Museum**: This museum houses one of the finest collections of medieval and Renaissance art in Germany, as well as Baroque and Impressionist masterpieces. It's a must-visit for those interested in art history.

- **Cologne Art Galleries**: The city's contemporary art scene thrives in areas like the Belgian Quarter and Ehrenfeld. Small galleries such as Boisserée Galerie and Galerie Karsten Greve exhibit cutting-edge works from both emerging and established artists.

Cologne's art fairs are also a highlight of the city's cultural calendar. Art Cologne, one of the world's oldest art fairs, takes place every spring, attracting artists, collectors, and dealers from across the globe.

Cologne Carnival (Karneval)

One of the most anticipated cultural events in Cologne is Karneval, or Carnival, often referred to as the "fifth season" by locals. Starting on November 11th at 11:11 AM, the Carnival season runs through winter and culminates in a week-long celebration leading up to Ash Wednesday in February or March. In 2025, Carnival will be in full swing from February 27 to March 4.

- **Rosenmontag (Rose Monday)**: This is the highlight of Carnival, with a massive parade featuring colorful floats, marching bands, and costumed participants. The parade route winds through Cologne's streets, and the festive spirit is contagious, with locals and visitors alike throwing candy and flowers.

- **Costumes and Traditions**: Dressing up in elaborate costumes is a big part of Cologne's Carnival culture. Whether you're dressed as a clown, pirate, or something more creative, you'll be welcomed into the celebrations.

- **Kölsch and Singing**: The local beer, Kölsch, flows freely during Carnival, and the streets are filled with traditional Carnival songs. These songs are sung in the local Kölsch dialect, and you'll quickly find yourself swept up in the infectious atmosphere of communal singing and dancing.

Carnival is a unique experience in Cologne, and in 2025, expect it to be bigger and more vibrant than ever, with street parties, balls, and events throughout the city.

Traditional Music and Performances

Cologne's rich musical tradition spans classical, contemporary, and folk music, with opportunities to experience both formal performances and spontaneous street music.

- **The Gürzenich Orchestra**: One of Germany's oldest symphony orchestras, the Gürzenich Orchestra regularly performs at the Kölner

Philharmonie, a modern concert hall located in the heart of the city. In 2025, the orchestra's schedule includes performances of classical works by composers like Beethoven, Mozart, and Brahms, as well as contemporary pieces.

- **Cologne Opera**: For opera lovers, the Cologne Opera presents a diverse range of productions, from classic operas to more avant-garde works. The 2025 season promises a mix of traditional operas like Verdi's *La Traviata* and modern pieces by living composers.

- **Folk Music and Kölsch Songs**: Throughout the year, you can find local bands performing traditional Kölsch music in pubs and during festivals. This lively, folk-influenced music is often sung in the Kölsch dialect and is a beloved part of Cologne's cultural heritage.

- **Street Performances**: Cologne is known for its vibrant street performance scene, particularly in areas like Alter Markt and the Rheinpromenade.

You'll often come across musicians, magicians, and dancers entertaining both locals and tourists.

Local Festivals and Events in 2025

Cologne hosts a variety of festivals and events throughout the year, celebrating everything from music and food to art and film. Here are some key events to look out for in 2025:

- **Cologne Lights (Kölner Lichter)**: Held every July, Cologne Lights is one of Europe's biggest music-synchronized fireworks displays. The event takes place along the Rhine River, and thousands of spectators gather to watch the stunning pyrotechnic show. In 2025, expect an even bigger display with accompanying live music performances and street festivities.

- **Cologne Pride (Christopher Street Day)**: One of the largest LGBTQ+ events in Europe, Cologne Pride takes place in July and features a colorful parade, parties, and cultural events. The festival promotes diversity, inclusion, and equality, and draws visitors from around the world.

- **Christmas Markets**: Cologne is famous for its Christmas markets, which attract millions of visitors each year. Starting in late November and running through December, these markets are spread across the city, with the most famous one being held in front of the Cologne Cathedral. In 2025, the Christmas markets will offer handmade gifts, mulled wine, traditional food, and festive entertainment.

- **Long Night of Museums**: Held annually in November, the Long Night of Museums allows visitors to explore Cologne's museums and galleries after hours. Special exhibitions, workshops, and performances are held, offering a unique cultural experience late into the night.

- **Cologne Marathon**: This major sporting event takes place every October and draws thousands of participants and spectators. In addition to the main marathon, there are also half-marathons and fun runs, making it a family-friendly event.

- **Cologne Carnival (Karneval)**

    Celebrated as the "fifth season," Cologne Carnival begins on November 11 and culminates in a week of festivities leading up to Ash Wednesday, with the main events taking place from February 27 to March 4, 2025. The highlight is the Rosenmontag parade on March 3, featuring colorful floats, costumes, and a lively atmosphere filled with music and celebration.

Whether you're visiting for a specific festival or just exploring the city, Cologne's cultural calendar for 2025 is packed with exciting events that showcase the city's vibrant traditions and modern spirit.

Chapter 8
Where to Eat and Drink in Cologne

Cologne is a culinary hotspot that offers a diverse array of dining experiences, ranging from traditional German fare to contemporary cuisine. The city is particularly known for its local specialties, craft beer scene, and vibrant café culture.

Traditional German Cuisine

Traditional German cuisine is characterized by hearty flavors and comforting dishes, often featuring locally sourced ingredients and time-honored recipes. Cologne's culinary scene is no exception, and there are many dishes you must try during your visit.

1. Sauerbraten: This pot roast is a classic German dish, typically made from beef marinated in a mixture of vinegar, water, and spices. It is slow-cooked to tenderness and served with red cabbage and potato dumplings. This dish can often be found in traditional restaurants throughout the city.

2. Kölsch Beer: As the local beer of Cologne, Kölsch is a light, pale ale served in small, cylindrical glasses known as Stange. The beer is brewed under strict guidelines and is a key part of the city's identity. Most restaurants and breweries offer Kölsch alongside their dishes, making it an essential part of the dining experience.

3. Himmel un Ääd: A beloved local specialty, this dish consists of mashed potatoes served with apple sauce, typically paired with blood sausage. The combination of savory and sweet flavors makes it a comforting and satisfying meal.

4. Rheinischer Kaviar (Rhenish Caviar): This unique dish features pickled herring and is typically served with boiled potatoes and rye bread. It's a must-try for those looking to experience traditional Rhenish cuisine.

5. Pork Knuckle (Eisbein): A hearty dish featuring a boiled pork knuckle served with sauerkraut and peas.

It's a popular choice for those seeking an authentic German meal.

Best Restaurants for Local Food

Cologne is home to numerous restaurants that celebrate the city's culinary heritage. Here are some of the best places to enjoy local food:

1. Päffgen: Located in the Belgian Quarter, this traditional brewpub is famous for its local dishes and atmosphere. The menu includes favorites like Himmel un Ääd and hearty sausages, all served with their house-made Kölsch. The cozy interior and friendly staff make it a great spot to relax and enjoy a meal.

2. Brauhaus Sion: Situated near the Old Town, this brewery restaurant offers generous portions of regional specialties. Their Sauerbraten and Pork Knuckle are particularly popular, and the lively atmosphere is perfect for groups looking to experience Cologne's vibrant dining scene.

3. Gaffel am Dom: Located right by the iconic Cologne Cathedral, this restaurant offers both traditional dishes and stunning views. The menu features classics like Rheinischer Kaviar and homemade potato dumplings, making it a must-visit for tourists and locals alike.

4. Zur Malzmühle: This traditional brewery is known for its authentic German cuisine and cozy ambiance. With dishes like Sauerbraten and Pork Knuckle served alongside their excellent Kölsch, it's an ideal place to experience Cologne's culinary culture.

5. Peters Brauhaus: Located in the heart of the city, this brewpub offers a wide variety of local dishes in a rustic setting. The menu includes everything from schnitzels to potato pancakes, all paired perfectly with their freshly brewed Kölsch.

6. Brauhaus Früh: A historic brewery that dates back to 1904, Früh is one of the most famous spots to enjoy traditional Cologne dishes. The restaurant is renowned for its hearty portions and vibrant atmosphere, making it a great place for both tourists and locals.

Craft Beer and Breweries

Cologne's craft beer scene has flourished in recent years, offering innovative brews that complement its traditional Kölsch culture. Here are some local breweries and craft beer bars worth exploring:

1. Friedrichshöfer: Known for its artisanal beers, this brewery focuses on small-batch production, offering tastings of various styles, including IPAs, stouts, and unique seasonal brews. The brewery's taproom provides a cozy setting to sample their creations.

2. Diebels: Situated in the Ehrenfeld district, Diebels is known for its innovative craft beers, including fruit-infused options and seasonal brews. The brewery frequently hosts events and tastings, allowing guests to explore a wide variety of flavors.

3. Braustelle: This microbrewery offers a range of craft beers, from IPAs to barrel-aged stouts, in a relaxed setting. Their rotating food truck provides a perfect pairing for your beer, making it a fun destination for food and drink lovers.

4. Hellers Brauhaus: A brewpub that combines traditional brewing techniques with modern flavors, Hellers offers both Kölsch and craft beer styles. The lively atmosphere, complete with outdoor seating, makes it a great place to enjoy a summer evening.

5. Brauhaus im Stadtgarten: Located in the picturesque Stadtgarten, this brewery is known for its craft beers and a delightful beer garden. The menu features a mix of traditional German dishes and innovative creations, making it an excellent choice for food and beer enthusiasts.

Cafés, Bakeries, and Sweets

Cologne's café culture is vibrant, with plenty of places to relax over coffee and indulge in delicious pastries and sweets. Here are some of the top cafés and bakeries to visit:

1. Café Rico: A cozy café in the Belgian Quarter, Café Rico serves excellent coffee and homemade cakes. It's a perfect spot for brunch or an afternoon treat, offering a relaxed atmosphere to unwind.

2. Bäckerei Schmitt: Known for its freshly baked goods, this bakery offers a variety of traditional German breads, pastries, and cakes. Their Kölner Zimtsterne (cinnamon stars) are a must-try during the holiday season.

3. Bäckerei Heinemann: A local favorite for its delicious pastries, cakes, and sandwiches, Heinemann is ideal for breakfast or a quick snack on the go. Their butter pretzels are particularly popular among locals.

4. Café Blum: A charming café with a variety of vegan and vegetarian options, including smoothies, salads, and vegan pastries. Café Blum is perfect for brunch or lunch, providing a welcoming atmosphere for all diners.

5. Törtchen Törtchen: A delightful patisserie known for its exquisite cakes and pastries, Törtchen Törtchen specializes in beautiful, artisanal sweets. Their tarts and éclairs are perfect for a sweet treat or a celebratory dessert.

6. Ditsch: Famous for its Pretzels, Ditsch has multiple locations throughout Cologne, serving up freshly baked pretzels that are perfect for a quick bite or a snack while exploring the city.

Vegan and Vegetarian Options

Cologne is increasingly becoming a hub for vegan and vegetarian cuisine, with many restaurants catering to plant-based diets. Here are some top spots to explore:

1. Veggie Bros: A popular vegan fast-food joint that offers a range of burgers, wraps, and bowls. This eatery provides delicious plant-based options that satisfy cravings without compromising on taste.

2. HANS IM GLÜCK: This stylish burger restaurant features a dedicated vegan menu, offering delicious plant-based burgers, salads, and sides. The modern ambiance makes it an inviting place for both vegans and non-vegans alike.

3. Café DREI: Known for its cozy atmosphere and commitment to sustainability, Café DREI offers a menu filled with vegetarian and vegan options, including hearty breakfasts, lunch bowls, and delicious coffee.

4. Tantalus: A vegetarian restaurant offering a creative menu inspired by global cuisine, Tantalus features a range of vegan options. The dishes are prepared with fresh ingredients and often change seasonally.

5. Kölner Kaffeemanufaktur: For coffee lovers seeking vegan options, this specialty coffee shop offers a range of plant-based pastries and snacks alongside expertly brewed coffee, perfect for a midday pick-me-up.

6. Buddha Bowl: This eatery focuses on healthy bowls made with fresh, organic ingredients. They offer a variety of vegan and vegetarian options, including grain bowls, salads, and smoothies, catering to health-conscious diners.

Chapter 9
Day Trips from Cologne

Cologne is ideally situated for exploring the surrounding regions, offering a variety of day trip options that cater to different interests. Whether you're interested in culture, nature, or amusement parks, here are some fantastic day trips to consider:

Bonn: The Birthplace of Beethoven

Just a short train ride from Cologne (approximately 30 minutes), Bonn is a city rich in history and cultural significance. Known as the birthplace of the famous composer Ludwig van Beethoven, Bonn is a charming destination for music lovers and history enthusiasts alike.

- **Beethoven-Haus**: Visit the museum located in the house where Beethoven was born. It features exhibits on his life, music, and the impact he had on the world of classical music.

- **Old Town (Altstadt)**: Stroll through Bonn's picturesque Old Town, where you can admire the beautiful architecture, including the Bonn Minster and the Old Town Hall. Quaint cafes and shops line the cobbled streets, providing the perfect backdrop for a leisurely day.

- **Poppelsdorf Palace and Botanical Gardens**: Explore the stunning Poppelsdorf Palace, a baroque building surrounded by lush gardens. The adjacent Botanical Gardens feature a diverse collection of plants and flowers, making it an excellent spot for a relaxing walk.

- **Rhein Promenade**: Take a leisurely walk along the Rhine River, where you can enjoy scenic views, have a picnic, or relax at one of the riverside cafes.

Düsseldorf: Art, Fashion, and the Rhine

Düsseldorf, located about 40 minutes by train from Cologne, is known for its vibrant arts scene, fashion industry, and modern architecture. A day trip to

Düsseldorf offers a mix of cultural experiences and shopping opportunities.

- **Königsallee (Kö)**: This famous shopping street is lined with luxury boutiques, designer stores, and charming cafes. It's a great place to indulge in some retail therapy or simply enjoy the atmosphere.

- **Altstadt (Old Town)**: Düsseldorf's Old Town is known as "the longest bar in the world" due to its many pubs and breweries. Here, you can try local specialties, including the famous Altbier (dark beer) brewed in the city.

- **Kunstsammlung Nordrhein-Westfalen**: Art enthusiasts will appreciate this impressive art collection, which houses works from the 20th century to contemporary art. Notable artists featured include Picasso and Klee.

- **Media Harbor**: Explore this modern waterfront area known for its striking architecture, including works by Frank Gehry. The Media Harbor offers a selection of trendy restaurants and bars, making it a perfect spot for dining with a view.

Phantasialand: Theme Park Fun

For families and thrill-seekers, Phantasialand is an exciting amusement park located about 30 minutes from Cologne by car. The park is known for its immersive themed areas and thrilling rides.

- **Themed Areas**: Phantasialand features several themed areas, each offering unique attractions, shows, and dining experiences. Notable themes include the Wild West, Asia, and the Berlin area, creating a diverse experience for visitors.

- **Exciting Rides**: The park is home to some of the most thrilling roller coasters and rides in Germany, including Taron, one of the fastest multi-launch coasters in the world, and Black Mamba, a thrilling inverted coaster.

- **Family-Friendly Attractions**: In addition to adrenaline-pumping rides, Phantasialand offers family-friendly attractions, including water rides, interactive shows, and playgrounds, ensuring there's something for everyone.

- **Dining and Shopping**: The park features a variety of dining options, from quick snacks to sit-down meals, as well as shops selling souvenirs and themed merchandise.

Exploring the Moselle Valley and Wine Regions

The Moselle Valley is a picturesque region known for its stunning landscapes, charming villages, and world-renowned wineries. It's an ideal destination for a day trip from Cologne, especially for wine lovers.

- **Scenic Views**: The Moselle River winds through lush vineyards and rolling hills, offering breathtaking views at every turn. Take a leisurely drive or bike ride along the river to fully appreciate the scenery.

- **Wine Tasting**: The region is famous for its Riesling wines. Many wineries offer tours and tastings, allowing you to sample a variety of local wines while learning about the winemaking process. Popular towns for wine tasting include Cochem and Bernkastel-Kues.

- **Charming Villages**: Explore the quaint villages along the Moselle River, such as Beilstein and Piesport. These towns are known for their half-timbered houses, cobbled streets, and welcoming atmospheres, perfect for leisurely strolls and photo opportunities.

- **Castle Visits**: The Moselle Valley is dotted with historic castles, including Reichsburg Cochem, which offers guided tours and panoramic views of the valley from its hilltop perch. Visiting these castles provides insight into the region's history and culture.

- **Hiking and Biking**: The Moselle region offers numerous hiking and biking trails, allowing you to immerse yourself in the natural beauty of the area. The Moselle Cycle Path is particularly popular among cyclists, providing a scenic route along the river.

Chapter 10
Shopping in Cologne

Cologne offers a vibrant shopping scene that caters to a wide range of tastes and budgets. From bustling shopping streets and modern malls to charming local markets and festive Christmas markets, there's something for everyone in this dynamic city.

Shopping Streets and Malls

Cologne boasts several popular shopping streets and malls that provide a diverse retail experience.

1. Schildergasse: One of the busiest shopping streets in Germany, Schildergasse is home to a variety of international and local brands. Here, you'll find everything from clothing and accessories to electronics and cosmetics. The street is pedestrian-friendly, making it ideal for leisurely strolls while exploring the numerous shops.

2. Hohe Straße: Adjacent to Schildergasse, Hohe Straße features a mix of high-street fashion retailers and unique boutiques. It's a great spot to find trendy clothing, shoes, and accessories. Many popular chain stores have outlets here, allowing shoppers to find a range of options.

3. Cologne Arcaden: Located in the Mülheim district, this modern shopping mall features over 100 shops, restaurants, and entertainment options. From fashion to electronics, the Cologne Arcaden offers a comprehensive shopping experience under one roof, making it a convenient choice for families.

4. Rhein-Center: Situated in the Bocklemünd area, the Rhein-Center is another large shopping mall featuring a wide variety of shops, cafes, and services. With its spacious layout and ample parking, it's a popular destination for both locals and visitors.

5. Altstadt: Cologne's Old Town (Altstadt) offers a charming shopping experience with its narrow streets and historic buildings. Here, you can find unique boutiques, artisan shops, and specialty stores selling handcrafted goods, antiques, and local products.

Local Markets

Exploring Cologne's local markets is a fantastic way to experience the city's culture while finding unique souvenirs.

1. Cologne Weekly Markets: Cologne hosts various weekly markets that offer fresh produce, local delicacies, and handmade crafts. The Alter Markt and Neumarkt are popular spots where you can immerse yourself in the lively atmosphere while sampling local treats.

2. Friesenplatz Market: Located near the trendy Friesenviertel, this market is known for its organic products, artisanal foods, and handmade crafts. It's a great place to pick up unique souvenirs, gourmet snacks, and local wines.

3. Cologne Cathedral Christmas Market: If you're visiting during the holiday season, the Christmas market held in the square in front of the Cologne Cathedral is a must-visit. You'll find stalls selling handmade ornaments, festive foods, and mulled wine, along with plenty of unique gifts to take home.

Luxury Brands and Designer Stores

For those looking to indulge in luxury shopping, Cologne has a selection of upscale boutiques and designer stores.

1. Königsallee (Kö): Known as one of Germany's most exclusive shopping streets, Königsallee is lined with high-end boutiques and luxury brand flagship stores. Here, you'll find designer names like Chanel, Gucci, Prada, and Louis Vuitton. It's the perfect place to shop for high fashion or simply enjoy window shopping amidst stunning architecture.

2. Schildergasse Luxury Stores: In addition to its high-street shops, Schildergasse also features several luxury boutiques. Brands like Michael Kors and Hugo Boss have stores in this area, offering a selection of upscale clothing and accessories.

3. Designer Outlet Köln: Located just outside the city center, this outlet mall features discounted designer brands, allowing shoppers to find deals on luxury items. With a range of stores from fashion to home goods, it's worth a visit for bargain hunters.

Cologne's Christmas Markets

Cologne's Christmas markets are among the most enchanting in Europe, drawing visitors from around the world. These festive markets typically open in late November and run through Christmas Eve, creating a magical atmosphere in the city.

1. Cologne Cathedral Christmas Market: Set against the stunning backdrop of the Cologne Cathedral, this market is the largest and most famous. Visitors can explore dozens of stalls selling traditional crafts, holiday decorations, and delicious food, including bratwurst, pretzels, and mulled wine. Live music and entertainment enhance the festive spirit.

2. Old Town Christmas Market: This charming market is located in the heart of the Old Town, featuring beautifully decorated stalls selling handmade goods, toys, and seasonal treats. The cozy atmosphere, complete with twinkling lights and festive decorations, makes it a delightful place to wander.

3. Harbor Christmas Market: Held at the historic Kölner Altstadt harbor, this market offers a unique maritime theme. Visitors can browse stalls set up on ships and enjoy live music and seasonal delicacies while taking in views of the Rhine River.

4. Heumarkt Christmas Market: Known for its impressive Christmas tree, this market features a wide variety of stalls selling local crafts, food, and beverages. It's a great place to find unique gifts and enjoy the festive atmosphere.

5. Alternative Christmas Market: For a more unconventional experience, the alternative Christmas market in Ehrenfeld features handmade crafts, vintage goods, and vegan food options, catering to those looking for something different.

Souvenirs from Cologne

When visiting Cologne, bringing home a souvenir is a great way to remember your trip and share a piece of the city with friends and family.

1. Kölsch Beer Glasses: These slender, cylindrical glasses are used to serve Kölsch, the local beer. They often come in sets and make for a practical yet stylish souvenir.

2. Chocolate from Cologne: Cologne is home to several renowned chocolatiers, such as Stollwerck. Consider bringing back artisanal chocolates or specialty chocolate bars as gifts.

3. Rheinischer Kaviar: This pickled herring delicacy is a local specialty that can be found in jars, making it a unique food souvenir to take home.

4. Köln Cathedral Miniature: A small replica of the iconic Cologne Cathedral (Kölner Dom) serves as a beautiful reminder of the city's architectural marvel.

5. Cologne Cathedral Postcards: Capture the stunning views of the Cathedral in postcard form to share with friends or as a keepsake.

6. Local Spices: Pick up some regional spices or seasoning blends from local markets to bring a taste of Cologne into your kitchen.

7. Traditional German Christmas Ornaments: If you visit during the holiday season, consider getting wooden ornaments or decorations inspired by local traditions.

8. Cologne's Perfume (4711): The famous Eau de Cologne 4711 is a classic fragrance originating from the city. A bottle makes for a fragrant and traditional gift.

9. Köln T-shirts and Apparel: Casual wear featuring Cologne's name or iconic symbols can be a fun way to remember your trip and wear it proudly.

10. Handcrafted Pottery: Look for locally made pottery or ceramic pieces that reflect the craftsmanship and culture of the region.

11. Art Prints: Purchase prints or artwork from local artists that capture Cologne's scenery or cultural landmarks.

12. Votive Candles: These candles are often beautifully crafted and can be found in local shops, perfect for creating a cozy atmosphere at home.

13. Magnetic Souvenirs: Fun magnets featuring Cologne landmarks are great for decorating your fridge and serve as a constant reminder of your visit.

14. Local Honey: Many markets sell honey produced by local beekeepers. It's a sweet way to bring back a taste of the region.

15. Craft Beer from Local Breweries: Pick up a few bottles of Kölsch or other craft beers produced by Cologne's breweries for friends or a personal tasting experience.

Chapter 11
Nightlife in Cologne

Cologne boasts a vibrant and diverse nightlife scene that caters to all tastes and preferences. Whether you're looking for a cozy pub, an energetic club, or a cultural experience, the city has something for everyone.

Best Bars and Pubs

Cologne's bars and pubs provide a welcoming atmosphere for both locals and visitors. Many are located in the city's Altstadt (Old Town) and surrounding neighborhoods, offering a mix of traditional and contemporary options.

1. Gaffel am Dom: Located near the Cologne Cathedral, this brewery is famous for its Kölsch beer. The spacious beer garden and traditional decor create a perfect setting to enjoy a pint of the local brew, paired with hearty German dishes.

2. Päffgen: A classic Kölsch brewery and pub, Päffgen has been serving locals since 1883. The lively atmosphere, wooden interior, and friendly staff make it a popular spot for an authentic Cologne experience.

3. The Bierhaus: Known for its extensive selection of beers, The Bierhaus is a great place to relax with friends. It features a laid-back atmosphere and often hosts events like quiz nights and live music.

4. Das kleine Bier: This cozy bar offers a wide range of craft beers, including local and international selections. The relaxed ambiance makes it a great place to unwind after a day of sightseeing.

Live Music Venues and Clubs

Cologne is a hub for live music and nightlife, with venues hosting everything from rock concerts to electronic dance parties.

1. Live Music Hall: This popular venue hosts a variety of live music acts, from up-and-coming artists to established bands. The energetic atmosphere and excellent acoustics make it a favorite among music lovers.

2. Club Bahnhof Ehrenfeld: A trendy spot for electronic music enthusiasts, this club hosts DJ sets and themed parties throughout the week. The industrial-style setting and impressive sound system create a memorable nightlife experience.

3. Luxor: Known for its eclectic mix of live music, Luxor features performances across various genres, including indie, rock, and electronic. The intimate venue allows for an up-close experience with the artists.

4. Stadtgarten: This cultural venue hosts regular concerts, open-air events, and parties. With its outdoor space and relaxed vibe, Stadtgarten is perfect for enjoying live music in the summer months.

Late-Night Dining and Entertainment

Cologne's culinary scene extends into the night, with various dining options available for late-night cravings.

1. Kölnisch Wasser: This restaurant offers a delightful late-night menu, including traditional German dishes and seasonal specialties. The warm ambiance and friendly service make it a great choice for a late dinner.

2. Früh am Dom: Located near the Cathedral, this brewery and restaurant serves delicious local cuisine and beer until late. It's a popular spot for both locals and tourists looking to enjoy hearty German fare.

3. Street Food Markets: Depending on the night, you may find food markets or street vendors offering a variety of delicious snacks. These markets often feature international cuisine, allowing you to sample different flavors as you explore the nightlife.

4. Late-Night Cafés: Several cafés in Cologne remain open late, serving coffee, pastries, and light meals. A cozy spot to unwind after a night out, these cafes often provide a relaxed atmosphere for conversation and relaxation.

Chapter 12
Cologne for Families

Cologne is a fantastic destination for families, offering a wide range of attractions and activities that cater to visitors of all ages. With its rich history, vibrant culture, and numerous parks, the city provides plenty of opportunities for family fun.

Family-Friendly Attractions

Cologne is home to a variety of attractions that appeal to children and adults alike. Here are some must-visit spots:

1. **Cologne Cathedral (Kölner Dom)**: This UNESCO World Heritage site is an iconic landmark that captivates visitors of all ages. Families can explore the cathedral's breathtaking architecture, including its impressive stained glass windows. Kids will enjoy the climb up to the viewing platform for stunning panoramic views of the city.

2. **Odysseum**: This interactive science and adventure museum is perfect for curious minds. Odysseum offers hands-on exhibits related to science, technology, and history, allowing kids to learn through play. The museum also features a 4D cinema and adventure zones, making it an engaging experience for the whole family.

3. **Cologne Zoo**: Home to over 700 animal species, Cologne Zoo provides a fun and educational day out for families. The zoo features spacious enclosures and interactive exhibits, including a petting zoo where kids can get up close to friendly animals. The nearby Flora und Botanischer Garten offers a beautiful botanical garden, perfect for a leisurely stroll after your zoo visit.

4. **Chocolate Museum (Schokoladenmuseum)**: A delightful treat for families, this museum offers an immersive experience into the world of chocolate. Kids can learn about the history of chocolate, see how it's made, and even taste samples from the chocolate fountain. The interactive exhibits and engaging displays make it a fun outing for all ages.

5. **Phantasialand**: Located just outside Cologne, this theme park offers thrilling rides, live shows, and immersive attractions for the whole family. With themed areas like "Berlin" and "Mexico," there's something for everyone, from roller coasters to family-friendly rides. The park is well-maintained and provides plenty of dining options, making it a fantastic day trip.

6. **Ludwig Museum**: While primarily an art museum, the Ludwig Museum hosts family-friendly workshops and activities that encourage creativity and exploration. Kids can participate in guided tours designed for younger audiences, helping them appreciate contemporary art in a fun and engaging way.

Parks and Playgrounds

Cologne is rich in green spaces and parks, providing ample opportunities for outdoor activities and relaxation.

1. **Rheinpark**: This expansive park along the Rhine River is perfect for families. With playgrounds, picnic areas, and stunning views of the river and the Cologne Cathedral, Rheinpark offers a relaxing environment. Kids can enjoy the large playground with climbing structures, slides, and swings, while parents can take a leisurely walk along the riverbanks.

2. **Volksgarten**: Another lovely park, Volksgarten features spacious lawns, flower gardens, and several playgrounds. It's a great spot for picnics and family outings. There's also a small lake where children can feed ducks and watch swans, adding to the park's charm.

3. **Friedenspark**: Located near the city center, Friedenspark is known for its beautiful landscaping and playgrounds. Families can enjoy a relaxing day out, and the park often hosts cultural events and performances, adding to the family-friendly atmosphere.

4. **Zoo Park**: Adjacent to the Cologne Zoo, Zoo Park features playgrounds and green spaces where families can relax. It's an excellent place for kids to burn off some energy after a day of exploring the zoo.

Child-Friendly Restaurants and Cafes

Cologne offers a variety of dining options that cater to families, making it easy to find kid-friendly meals.

1. **Päffgen**: This traditional Kölsch brewery is welcoming to families, offering a relaxed atmosphere and a menu featuring hearty German cuisine. Kids can enjoy classic dishes like schnitzel or sausages, and the brewery often has high chairs available.

2. **Bergischer Hof**: Located in the Old Town, this restaurant serves traditional German food in a family-friendly environment. The menu includes options for children, ensuring everyone finds something they enjoy.

3. **Café de Paris**: This café is known for its casual atmosphere and diverse menu, including

sandwiches, salads, and pastries. It's an excellent spot for a light lunch or afternoon snack, with plenty of kid-friendly options.

4. **Kaffeekommune**: A cozy café that serves excellent coffee and delicious baked goods, Kaffeekommune is also a great place for families. They offer pastries and snacks that kids will love, and the laid-back atmosphere makes it easy to relax.

5. **L'Oliva**: This Italian restaurant features a family-friendly menu, with options like pizza and pasta that are sure to please kids. The warm and inviting ambiance makes it a great spot for families to enjoy a meal together.

Tips for Traveling with Kids

Traveling with kids can be a rewarding experience, and here are some tips to make your trip to Cologne enjoyable:

1. **Plan Ahead**: Research family-friendly attractions, dining options, and activities in advance to create a

balanced itinerary that includes something for everyone.

2. **Public Transportation**: Cologne has an excellent public transportation system, including trams and buses, making it easy to navigate the city with kids. Consider getting a family day pass for unlimited travel, which is both convenient and cost-effective.

3. **Pack Essentials**: Bring along snacks, water, and any essential items your child may need throughout the day. This will help keep everyone happy and energized as you explore.

4. **Choose Accommodations Wisely**: Look for family-friendly hotels or accommodations that offer amenities like cribs, play areas, or family suites. This can make your stay more comfortable and enjoyable.

5. **Take Breaks**: Be sure to schedule breaks throughout your day to rest and recharge. Parks and playgrounds are great spots for kids to run around while parents can relax.

6. **Engage Kids in Planning**: Involve your children in the planning process by asking them what they'd like to see or do. This can help them feel more excited about the trip and invested in the experiences.

7. **Have Fun!**: Remember that travel is an adventure, so embrace the unexpected and enjoy the time spent together as a family. Capture moments with photos and create lasting memories during your Cologne visit.

Chapter 13
Practical Information

Currency and Etiquette in Cologne

When visiting Cologne, understanding the local currency and etiquette can enhance your travel experience.

Currency

Cologne, as part of Germany, uses the euro (€) as its official currency. Here are essential points about the euro and managing your money while in Cologne:

1. **Currency Exchange**: Euros can be exchanged at banks, currency exchange offices, and ATMs throughout the city. Most banks offer favorable exchange rates, but be cautious of any service fees that may apply. Airports and hotels typically charge higher rates, so it's best to avoid exchanging large amounts there.

2. **ATMs**: Automated Teller Machines (ATMs) are widely available in Cologne, particularly in tourist areas, shopping districts, and near public transport

stations. Most ATMs accept major international debit and credit cards, but it's advisable to check with your bank regarding international withdrawal fees beforehand.

3. **Cash vs. Card**: While credit and debit cards (especially Visa and Mastercard) are accepted in many establishments, cash is still commonly used in Cologne, particularly in smaller shops, restaurants, and local markets. Carrying some cash is recommended to avoid inconveniences.

4. **Coins**: The euro is divided into coins: 1 cent, 2 cents, 5 cents, 10 cents, 20 cents, 50 cents, €1, and €2. You may need coins for public transport, vending machines, or small purchases.

Etiquette

Understanding local etiquette is vital for making a good impression and enjoying your time in Cologne. Here are some essential tips:

1. **Greetings**: Germans generally greet with a firm handshake and direct eye contact. A friendly "Hallo" or "Guten Tag" is appropriate. In more informal settings, such as among friends or younger people, "Hi" is also acceptable.

2. **Politeness**: Being polite is valued in German culture. Use "Bitte" (please) and "Danke" (thank you) frequently. If you're unsure of what to say, err on the side of formality until you gauge the situation.

3. **Dining Etiquette**: When dining out, it is customary to wait for everyone to be served before starting to eat. It's also polite to keep your hands on the table (but not your elbows) while dining. Tipping (around 5% to 10% of the bill) is common, but you should add it to the total when paying the bill rather than leaving it on the table.

4. **Public Transport**: If you are using public transportation, it's courteous to offer your seat to elderly passengers or those with disabilities. When using escalators, stand on the right side to allow others to pass on the left.

5. **Photography**: Be mindful when taking photos, especially of people or private properties. Always ask for permission if you're photographing someone directly, and be respectful of signage prohibiting photography in certain areas (like museums or galleries).

6. **Dress Code**: Germans generally dress smartly and appropriately for the occasion. While casual attire is accepted in most places, it's best to avoid overly casual clothing when dining in nicer restaurants or attending cultural events.

7. **Punctuality**: Being on time is important in German culture. Arriving late can be considered rude, so always aim to be punctual for meetings, meals, and events.

8. **Personal Space**: Germans value personal space and may stand at a distance during conversations. Avoid standing too close unless you have established a comfortable rapport.

Tipping Etiquette

Tipping in Germany is generally appreciated but not mandatory. Here's a breakdown of tipping etiquette to help you navigate this aspect of your visit to Cologne:

1. Restaurants and Cafés: In restaurants and cafes, it is customary to round up the bill or add about 5% to 10% for good service. For example, if your bill is €18, you might leave €20. If you receive exceptional service, consider tipping 10% to 15%.

2. Bars and Pubs: At bars, it's common to round up the total amount. If you order a drink that costs €4.50, you can leave €5 and say "stimmt so" (which means "keep the change").

3. Taxis: For taxi drivers, rounding up the fare to the nearest euro is appreciated. If the fare is €12.80, giving the driver €15 is a friendly gesture.

4. Hotels: For hotel staff, it is customary to tip porters about €1 to €2 per bag. For housekeeping, consider leaving €1 to €3 per night, depending on the level of service.

5. Cultural Venues: If you attend performances at theaters, concerts, or other cultural venues, tipping is generally not expected. However, you can show appreciation by giving a small amount (like €1 or €2) to musicians or performers if you feel inclined.

6. Other Services: In beauty salons, spas, and other personal services, it is also polite to leave a tip of around 5% to 10%, depending on your satisfaction with the service provided.

Language and Useful Phrases in Cologne

Cologne is located in Germany, where the official language is German. However, many residents, especially in the tourism and service sectors, also speak English. While you can navigate the city using English, learning a few basic German phrases can enhance your experience and show respect for the local culture. Here's a breakdown of the language landscape and some useful phrases for your visit.

Language Overview

1. **German**: The predominant language spoken in Cologne is Standard German (Hochdeutsch). This is the formal language used in education, media, and official communications.

2. **Cologne Dialect**: In addition to Standard German, many locals speak Kölsch, a dialect specific to the Cologne area. While Kölsch may be challenging for non-native speakers, it's a charming part of the city's culture, especially during local festivals and casual conversations.

3. **English**: Due to the city's status as a major tourist destination and its proximity to international business centers, many people in Cologne, particularly younger generations, can communicate effectively in English. You will find that signs in public areas, menus, and information boards often include English translations.

Useful Phrases

Knowing a few key phrases in German can help you interact with locals, navigate your way around the city, and enrich your travel experience. Here are some essential phrases to get you started:

1. **Greetings and Introductions**:

    - **Hallo!** – Hello!

    - **Guten Morgen!** – Good morning!

    - **Guten Tag!** – Good day!

    - **Guten Abend!** – Good evening!

    - **Gute Nacht!** – Good night!

    - **Wie geht's?** – How are you?

    - **Ich heiße...** – My name is... (e.g., Ich heiße Anna.)

    - **Freut mich, Sie kennenzulernen!** – Nice to meet you!

2. **Basic Courtesy**:

    - **Bitte.** – Please.

- **Danke!** – Thank you!
- **Vielen Dank!** – Thank you very much!
- **Entschuldigung.** – Excuse me / Sorry.
- **Könnte ich bitte die Rechnung haben?** – Could I please have the bill?

3. **Directions and Assistance**:

- **Wo ist…?** – Where is…? (e.g., Wo ist der Bahnhof? – Where is the train station?)
- **Ich habe eine Frage.** – I have a question.
- **Sprechen Sie Englisch?** – Do you speak English?
- **Könnten Sie das bitte wiederholen?** – Could you please repeat that?
- **Ich verstehe nicht.** – I don't understand.

4. **Dining and Shopping**:

- **Ich hätte gerne…** – I would like… (e.g., Ich hätte gerne ein Bier. – I would like a beer.)

- **Haben Sie eine Speisekarte auf Englisch?** – Do you have a menu in English?
- **Das kostet...** – That costs... (e.g., Das kostet 10 Euro.)
- **Kann ich mit Karte bezahlen?** – Can I pay by card?

5. **Travel and Transportation**:
   - **Wo kann ich ein Ticket kaufen?** – Where can I buy a ticket?
   - **Wann fährt der nächste Zug nach...?** – When does the next train to... leave? (e.g., Wann fährt der nächste Zug nach Berlin?)
   - **Ich möchte ein Ticket nach... kaufen.** – I would like to buy a ticket to...

6. **Emergencies**:
   - **Hilfe!** – Help!
   - **Ich brauche einen Arzt.** – I need a doctor.

- **Wo ist die nächste Apotheke?** – Where is the nearest pharmacy?

- **Rufen Sie die Polizei!** – Call the police!

Tips for Communication

1. **Polite Tone**: Germans value politeness and directness in communication. Using "Bitte" and "Danke" frequently is essential for showing respect.

2. **Speaking Slowly**: If you attempt to speak German, don't worry about making mistakes. Most locals appreciate the effort. If you're struggling, feel free to switch to English, as many will be willing to assist.

3. **Use Simple Phrases**: Stick to basic phrases and vocabulary, especially if you are not confident in your German language skills. Many locals will understand simple phrases even if you struggle with pronunciation.

4. **Learn Basic Numbers**: Familiarizing yourself with numbers in German can be helpful, especially

when dealing with prices, public transport, or directions.

Safety Tips for Travelers in Cologne

Cologne is generally considered a safe city for travelers, but like any urban destination, it's essential to take certain precautions to ensure a worry-free experience.

1. Stay Aware of Your Surroundings

- **Be Alert**: Keep an eye on your belongings, especially in crowded areas such as public transport, tourist attractions, and markets. Pickpocketing can occur in busy places.

- **Avoid Distractions**: When using your phone or looking at a map, try to stay aware of your surroundings. This helps you avoid accidents or becoming an easy target for theft.

2. Use Reliable Transportation

- **Public Transport**: Cologne has an efficient public transportation system, including trams and buses. Stick to well-lit and populated stations, especially at night.

- **Taxis and Ride-Sharing**: If you need to travel late at night, consider using licensed taxis or reputable ride-sharing services like Uber. Always check the driver's credentials before getting in.

3. Keep Your Valuables Secure

- **Use Anti-Theft Bags**: Consider using bags with zippers or anti-theft features to protect your valuables. Carry bags in front of you and never leave them unattended.

- **Separate Your Cash and Cards**: Keep your cash, cards, and important documents in different locations (like a money belt or secure pocket) to minimize loss if theft occurs.

4. Be Cautious at Night

- **Stick to Well-Lit Areas**: When walking around at night, avoid dark and isolated areas. Stay in well-populated places where there are other people around.

- **Travel in Groups**: If possible, travel with friends or family, especially at night. There's safety in numbers, and it can enhance your experience.

5. Respect Local Customs and Laws

- **Public Behavior**: Be respectful of local customs and behaviors. Loud, disruptive actions might attract unwanted attention or upset locals.

- **Alcohol Consumption**: Enjoy Cologne's famous beers responsibly. Public drinking is allowed, but excessive drunkenness can lead to unsafe situations.

Emergency Contacts and Services in Cologne

Knowing whom to contact in case of an emergency can provide peace of mind during your travels.

1. Emergency Numbers

- **Police**: Dial **110** for police assistance in emergencies. This number is used for reporting crimes or if you feel threatened.

- **Ambulance and Medical Emergencies**: Dial **112** for medical emergencies or if someone requires immediate medical assistance.

- **Fire Department**: The fire department can also be reached by calling **112**. This number covers all emergency services, including fire-related incidents.

2. Local Hospitals and Clinics

- **Universitätsklinikum Köln**: A major university hospital located in Cologne, providing comprehensive medical services. Address: Zülpicher Str. 9, 50937 Köln, Germany.

- **Klinik für Innere Medizin und Gastroenterologie**: Specializes in internal medicine and gastroenterology. Address: Hohenstaufenring 20, 50674 Köln, Germany.

- **Emergency Services**: If you need medical attention after hours, hospitals typically have an emergency department. Look for signs indicating "Notaufnahme" (emergency admission) at hospitals.

3. Finding Help

- **Tourist Information Centers**: If you find yourself in need of assistance, the local tourist information centers can be helpful. They can provide information on local services and emergency contacts.

- **Local Authorities**: If you need help in a non-emergency situation (like a lost item), visit the nearest police station. The main station in Cologne is located at Kaiser-Wilhelm-Ring 30, 50672 Köln, Germany.

4. Consulates and Embassies

- If you are a foreign traveler and need assistance, locate your country's embassy or consulate in Germany. They can provide support for lost passports, legal issues, or other emergencies.

CONCLUSION

As you wrap up your exploration of Cologne, it's important to reflect on the city's rich history, vibrant culture, and the diverse experiences it offers. Whether you're drawn to its stunning architecture, lively festivals, or culinary delights, Cologne has something for every traveler.

Final Thoughts

1. **Embrace the Local Culture**: Cologne is known for its friendly and welcoming atmosphere. Engaging with locals, participating in cultural events, and trying traditional dishes will enrich your experience. Don't hesitate to strike up conversations with residents; you may gain valuable insights and recommendations.

2. **Explore Beyond the Tourist Spots**: While the major attractions are a must-see, don't forget to venture off the beaten path. Discover hidden gems, quaint neighborhoods, and local markets that

provide a more authentic experience of the city. Cologne's charm often lies in its lesser-known corners.

3. **Seasonal Experiences**: Depending on when you visit, take advantage of seasonal events and activities. From Christmas markets in winter to outdoor festivals in summer, each season offers unique experiences that highlight Cologne's cultural vibrancy.

4. **Plan for Flexibility**: While it's helpful to have an itinerary, allow for spontaneity during your visit. Some of the best memories come from unplanned adventures or recommendations from locals. Be open to changing your plans based on what you discover.

Recommendations

1. **Try Local Cuisine**: Make it a point to savor Cologne's culinary offerings. Don't miss the chance to try Himmel un Ääd (Heaven and Earth), Reibekuchen (potato pancakes), and local Kölsch

beer. Visit traditional Brauhaus (breweries) for an authentic dining experience.

2. **Participate in Festivals**: If your visit coincides with local festivals, such as Karneval or Christopher Street Day, immerse yourself in the festivities. These events offer a unique glimpse into Cologne's cultural identity and community spirit.

3. **Utilize Public Transport**: Cologne has an efficient public transportation system, making it easy to navigate the city and surrounding areas. Consider purchasing a day pass for unlimited travel on trams and buses, allowing you to explore comfortably.

4. **Take Day Trips**: Cologne's strategic location makes it an excellent base for day trips. Explore nearby cities like Bonn, Düsseldorf, and the scenic Moselle Valley. Each offers unique attractions and experiences worth your time.

5. **Engage with Art and History**: Visit local museums and galleries to deepen your understanding of Cologne's artistic and historical heritage. The Roman-Germanic Museum and

Museum Ludwig are excellent choices for art and history enthusiasts.

6. **Safety First**: As with any travel destination, stay aware of your surroundings, secure your belongings, and familiarize yourself with emergency contacts. Cologne is generally safe, but taking precautions ensures a worry-free visit.

FAQs

1. **What is the best time to visit Cologne?**

    - **Best Time**: The ideal time to visit Cologne is during the spring (April to June) and early fall (September to October) when the weather is mild, and there are fewer tourists. However, if you enjoy festive atmospheres, visiting during the Christmas season to experience the Christmas markets is also a great option.

2. **Is Cologne a safe city for tourists?**

    - **Safety**: Yes, Cologne is generally considered a safe city for tourists. Like any urban area, it's important to be cautious and aware of your surroundings, especially in crowded places. Petty crimes such as pickpocketing can occur, so it's advisable to keep your belongings secure.

3. **What are the must-see attractions in Cologne?**

    - **Top Attractions**: Key attractions include the Cologne Cathedral (Kölner Dom), Hohenzollern Bridge, the Roman-Germanic Museum, and the charming Old Town (Altstadt). Don't forget to take a stroll along the Rhine River and visit local parks and gardens.

4. **What local dishes should I try?**

    - **Local Cuisine**: Be sure to try traditional dishes such as **Himmel unÄäd** (a dish made of apples and potatoes), **Reibekuchen** (potato pancakes), and the famous **Kölsch** beer. Cologne also has a rich pastry tradition, so don't miss out on local bakeries.

5. **Is English widely spoken in Cologne?**

    - **Language**: Yes, many people in Cologne, especially in the hospitality and tourism sectors, speak English. However, learning a few basic German phrases can enhance your experience and show respect for the local culture.

Myths

1. **Cologne is Just About the Cathedral**:

    - **Myth**: While the Cologne Cathedral is a prominent landmark, many believe that it's the only significant attraction in the city.

    - **Reality**: Cologne boasts a rich cultural scene, diverse neighborhoods, vibrant festivals, and numerous museums that showcase its history and arts. The city offers much more beyond its iconic cathedral.

2. **Cologne is Not Family-Friendly**:

    - **Myth**: Some travelers think that Cologne lacks family-oriented activities.

    - **Reality**: Cologne is quite family-friendly, with many attractions suitable for children, including parks, zoos, and interactive museums. Events like the Cologne Carnival also engage families, making it a great destination for all ages.

3. **All Germans Are Rigid and Unfriendly**:

    - **Myth**: A common stereotype is that Germans, including those in Cologne, are serious and unfriendly.

    - **Reality**: Cologne residents are known for their warm and welcoming nature. The city's Carnival and local festivals reflect the jovial spirit of its people, and visitors often find locals eager to engage and share their culture.

4. **Kölsch is Just for Locals**:

    - **Myth**: Some believe that only locals can enjoy Kölsch beer or that it's exclusive to Cologne.

    - **Reality**: Kölsch is a delightful beer enjoyed by both locals and visitors. It's served in small glasses and is a key part of the local culinary experience. Visitors are encouraged to taste and enjoy it while exploring the city.

5. **Cologne is a Small City**:

    - **Myth**: Some think that because Cologne is not as internationally known as cities like Berlin or Munich, it's a small and insignificant place.

    - **Reality**: Cologne is Germany's fourth-largest city, with a diverse population and a rich history. It offers a wide array of activities, attractions, and cultural experiences, making it a vibrant metropolis worth exploring.

Dear Valued Readers,

Thank you for choosing **"Cologne Travel Guide 2025"** as your companion on your journey through this enchanting city. I hope this guide has provided you with valuable insights and enhanced your exploration of Cologne's stunning architecture, vibrant neighborhoods, and rich cultural heritage.

Your feedback and reviews are incredibly important to me. If you found this guide helpful and enjoyed discovering Cologne alongside it, please consider leaving an honest review on Amazon. Your reviews not only inspire me to continue creating meaningful content but also help fellow travelers make informed decisions.

I sincerely hope that this guide has enriched your Cologne experience, allowing you to immerse yourself in the city's unique charm, historical landmarks, and local flavors in a memorable way.

Wishing you a safe and rewarding journey. Embrace the wonders of Cologne, dive into its vibrant culture, and savor every moment of your travel experience.

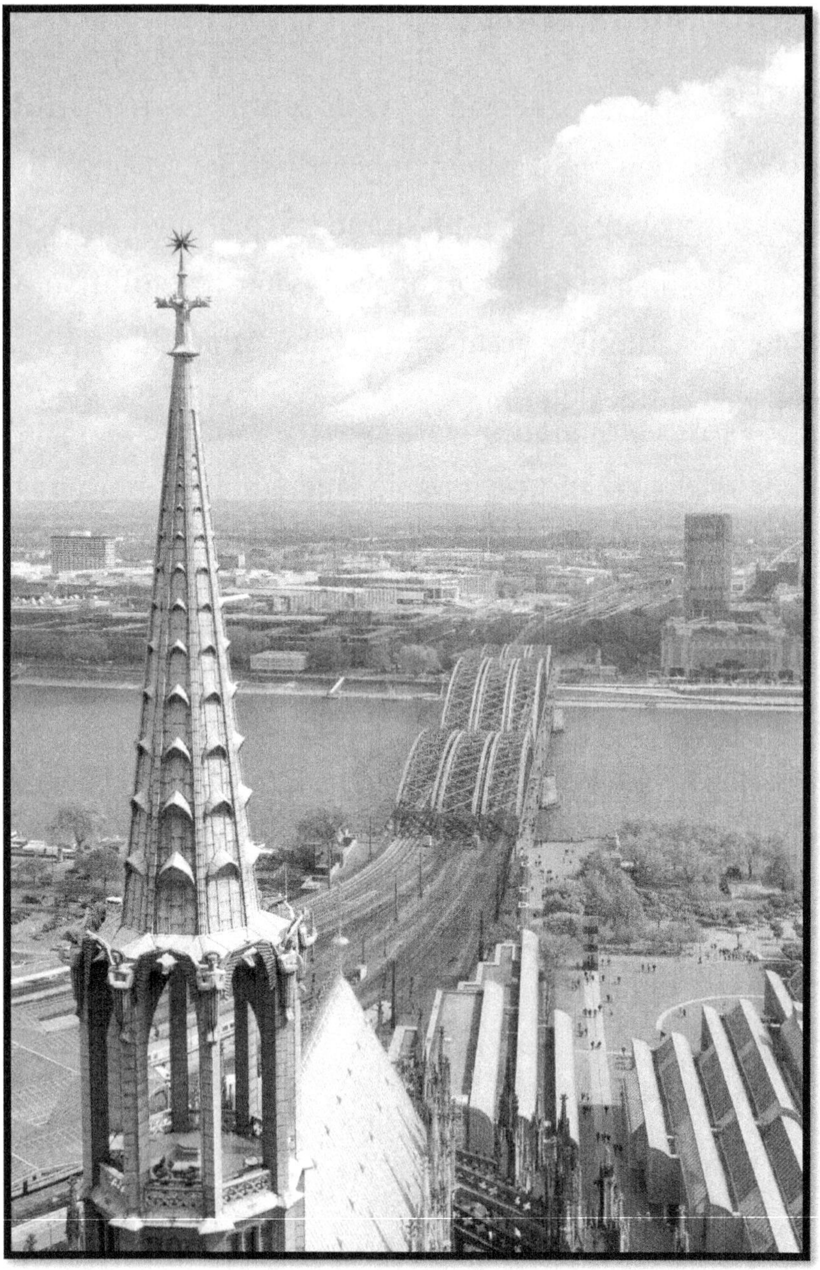

Thank You Once Again, And Happy Travels!

Printed in Great Britain
by Amazon